NOËL
COWARD

IN HIS OWN WORDS

NOËL COWARD

IN HIS OWN WORDS

::: ::: :::

Compiled and introduced by
Barry Day

Methuen

Published by Methuen 2004

3 5 7 9 10 8 6 4 2

Original version (entitled *Noël Coward: A Life in Quotes*) first
published in Great Britain in 1999 by Metro Books (an imprint of
Metro Publishing Limited)

This revised and enlarged version published by
Methuen Publishing Limited
215 Vauxhall Bridge Road
London SW1V 1EJ
www.methuen.co.uk

Methuen Publishing Limited Reg. No. 3543167

ISBN 0 413 77441 4

Extracts from Coward's plays, verse, lyrics and autobiography
reproduced by association with Methuen Publishing Limited.

The author and publishers are grateful to Weidenfeld & Nicolson
for permission to reprint extracts from the *Diaries*.

Caricatures on pp. 53 and 100 by Clive Francis. Illustration on
p. 60 by Marc reproduced by kind permission.

Every effort has been made to trace the current copyright holders
of the extracts and illustrations included in this work. The publishers
apologise for any unintended omissions and would be pleased to
receive any information that would enable them to amend any
inaccuracies or omissions in future editions.

A CIP catalogue for this title is available from the British Library.

Typeset by SX Composing DTP, Rayleigh, Essex

Printed and bound in Great Britain
by Mackays of Chatham plc, Chatham, Kent

How invaluable it would be . . . if just once, for a brief spell, I could see myself clearly from the outside, as others saw me. How helpful it would be, moving so continually across the public vision, to know what that vision really observed, to note objectively what it was in my personality that moved some people to like and applaud me and aroused in others such irritation and resentment. How salutary it would be to watch the whole performance through from the front of the house, to see to what extent the mannerisms were effective and note when and where they should be cut down.

Future Indefinite (1954)

How invaluable it would be . . . if just once, for a brief
spell, I could see myself clearly from the outside, as others
saw me. How helpful it would be, moving so continually
across the public vision, to know what that vision really
observed, to note objectively what it was in my personality
that moved some people to like and applaud me and
aroused in others such irritation and resentment. How
salutary it would be to watch the whole performance
through from the front of the house, to see to what extent
the mannerisms were effective and note when and where
they should be cut down.

Future Indefinite (1954)

Quotes *on* Coward

The Congreve of our time.

Arnold Bennett

Destiny's tot.

Alexander Woollcott

A sort of Marconi of the artistic world.

Ruby Miller (Mrs Max Darewski)

He is simply a phenomenon and one that is unlikely to
occur ever again in theatre history – actor, director,
dramatist unrivalled this century.

Terence Rattigan

. . . he was a master because he so bravely and brilliantly
made use of the sentimental as well as the comic and
because under that clipped precision, there was tenderness,
particularly towards the unimportant, the bit parts and the
failures.

Sir John Betjeman at the thanksgiving service (1973)

(He is) his own invention and contribution to the twentieth
century.

John Osborne

There are probably greater painters than Noël, greater
novelists than Noël, greater librettists, greater composers of
music, greater singers, greater dancers, greater comedians,
greater tragedians, greater stage producers, greater film
directors, greater cabaret artists, greater TV stars. If there
are, they are fourteen different people. Only one man
combined all fourteen different labels – The Master.

Lord Louis Mountbatten at Noël's 70th birthday party (1969)

Even the youngest of us will know, in fifty years' time,
precisely what is meant by 'a very Noël Coward sort of
person'.

Kenneth Tynan

CONTENTS

⁘   ⁘   ⁘

INTRODUCTION The Word According to Coward xi

PART ONE 'Why Must the Show Go On?' 1

PART TWO 'A Marvellous Party' 45

PART THREE 'Mad Dogs and Englishmen' 63

PART FOUR 'Sail Away' 75

PART FIVE 'If Love Were All . . .' 97

PART SIX 'Sigh No More' 119

PART SEVEN Envoi: 'I'll See You Again' 141

INTRODUCTION

The Word According to Coward

⸬ ⸬ ⸬

Did Noël Coward use the words – or did the words use him?

Certainly, you'd be hard put to name anyone in the twentieth century who employed the English language with the same precision, concision and consistency as he did. And his range was remarkable. In the dialogue of his plays, in verse, song lyrics, essays, stories, letters, auto-biography, interviews – and perhaps most particularly in private conversation – words were his weapons, and 'wordsmith' both his occupation and his preoccupation.

An essentially private person for so public a persona, he consistently used the words to create an image behind which he could hide his more vulnerable emotions. So effective was this defence mechanism that Coward has rarely been given the credit for even possessing ordinary sensibilities – although he provided a clue to the contrary in one of his plays. In *Shadow Play* he has Gertrude Lawrence say: 'Small talk, a lot of small talk with other thoughts going on behind.' The small talk and the apparent frivolity are what we employ when to say what we really *mean* would prove too painful.

American novelist Peter de Vries once skewered one of his own characters by saying that 'on the surface he was deep – but deep down he was shallow'. Precisely the opposite was true of Noël Coward but, ironically, it was largely the posthumous publication of his *Diaries* and a study of his private papers that provided the portrait with its present light and shade.

Coward was a curious man – in the strict sense of that word. He was fascinated by the people with whom he shared the planet, by the feelings they apparently had in common and the behaviour – particularly the patterns of speech – that differentiated them, so that the same words from different speakers could convey quite different meanings. And everything he saw and heard he recorded.

One speech in *Present Laughter* (1939) will serve as an example. The actor Garry Essendine is making stilted small talk with the aspiring young playwright Roland Maule:

> GARRY: You've come all the way from Uckfield?
> ROLAND: It isn't very far.
> GARRY: Well, it sort of *sounds* far, doesn't it?
> ROLAND: (*defensively*) It's quite near Lewes.
> GARRY: Then there's nothing to worry about, is there?

A sociological thesis couldn't define the two characters more precisely.

Coward is generally considered a man who lived in and for the moment. In fact, he never forgot a humble past and constantly recreated it in his depiction (often more nostalgically affectionate than realistic) of working-class life. He was also concerned – increasingly so as the years went by – with the purpose of life. Among the earliest musings he privately committed to youthful paper, he debates with himself the value of religion. In public, the instinctive barrier of words is erected.

Did he believe in God?, David Frost once asked him in

a television interview. 'We've never been intimate – but maybe we do have a few things in common,' Noël replied, lighting the ever-present cigarette and disappearing behind a cloud of smoke.

In a later interview he was asked for the one valedictory word he felt would sum up the play that had been his life. He bought himself a little time by pondering aloud the risk of sounding corny before settling on: 'LOVE . . . To know that you are among people whom you love and who love you. That has made all the successes wonderful – much more wonderful than they'd have been anyway. And I don't think there's anything more to be said after that.'

Seen in this light, Coward's use of words is significantly different from that of the two writers with whom he is most often compared. A Wilde epigram may have a greater surface shine, but drop it and all you are left with are fragments. Pick up one by Shaw and you may well cut yourself, for it lacks kindness. Coward is altogether more comfortable company because his is the language of the good conversationalist and the kind man; his *bons mots* deal with the stuff of all our lives, and perhaps what defines him most is that you feel you have thought these thoughts and might have expressed many of them yourself – if only the words had fallen in the right order.

In this collection I have naturally included many of the 'classic' Coward lines but I have also delved into the private papers and unpublished material for lines that – even out of context – show a mind in the making and the emergence of themes he would reorchestrate and refine as the years went by. Where possible I have attributed the quotations to their specific context but inevitably – as with all the great wits – some have become part of the legend by word of mouth. Coward himself summed up the dilemma best when he declared: 'I'm naturally a witty man. I have been and doubtless I always shall be. In my time I've said some noteworthy and exceptionally memorable things. If the remarks with which I am credited – and never made – are really good, I acknowledge them. I generally work myself into the belief that I originally said them.'

This collection reveals more than merely a unique wit – the precious commodity he always felt should be 'a glorious treat like caviar', not 'spread about like marmalade'. It depicts a man of depth, compassion and London pride. After the 'cocktails and laughter' there was infinitely more than just 'a talent to amuse'.

Barry Day
2004

PART ONE

⣿ ⣿ ⣿

'Why Must the Show Go On?'

To Coward, the theatre was virtually a religion, a 'temple of illusion', and he could not bear to see that temple desecrated by philistines, either from within or from without. Typically, his punishment was ridicule.

Genuine lack of talent always appalled him, as did some of the theatre's more arcane traditions. After half a century of watching gallant 'troupers', young or old, dragging themselves through their 'Laugh, Clown, Laugh' routines to ensure that the show went on regardless, he decided he had finally had enough and, in a song in his Café de Paris cabaret act in the early 1950s, he posed the question no one was meant to ask:

> *Why must the show go on?*
> *It can't be all that indispensable,*
> *To me it really isn't sensible*
> *On the whole*
> *To play a leading role*
> *While fighting those tears you can't control,*
> *Why kick up your legs*
> *When draining the dregs*
> *Of sorrow's bitter cup?*
> *Because you have read*
> *Some idiot has said*
> *'The Curtain must go up!'*

'Why Must the Show Go On?' (1954)

Not that his own career ran entirely smoothly:

> I partnered a girl named Eileen Dennis, and we were engaged by the Elysée Restaurant (now the Café de Paris) to appear during dinner and supper.

A slow waltz, a tango, and a rather untidy one-step made up our programme. Later, owing to popular demand (from Eileen Dennis's mother), we introduced a *pierrot fantasia* for which we changed into cherry-coloured sateen and tulle ruffs. No South African millionaires threw diamond sunbursts at Eileen's feet. We were neither of us ever invited to appear naked out of pies at private supper parties, in fact the whole engagement from the point of view of worldly experience was decidedly disappointing.

Present Indicative (1937)

MR. NOËL COWARD MAKING MENTAL NOTES
FOR THE FIRST PART OF "CAVALCADE."

His début came at a ridiculously early age and he would look back on his younger self with awed objectivity:

> I was a brazen, odious little prodigy, over-pleased
> with myself and precocious to a degree.
>
> Present Indicative (1937)

⠿　⠿　⠿

> Miss Joan Carroll and Mr. Noël Coward as the
> Toadstool and the Mushroom headed delightfully a
> little troupe of various small and engaging fungi.
>
> The Times reviewing An Autumn Idyll (1912)

Reflecting on an early performance:

> I am certain that, could my adult self have been
> present . . . he would have crept out, at the first coy
> gurgle, and been mercifully sick outside.
>
> Present Indicative (1937)

⠿　⠿　⠿

> *An infant prodigy of nine*
> *Is shoved upon the stage in white.*
> *She starts off in a dismal whine*
> *About a Dark and Stormy night,*
> *A burglar whose heart is true,*
> *Despite his wicked looking face!*
> *And what a little child can do*
> *To save her Mama's jewel case!*
>
> Concert Types (1917)

⠿　⠿　⠿

I was a talented child, God knows, and when washed
and smarmed down a bit, passably attractive; but I
was, I believe, one of the worst boy actors ever
inflicted on the paying public.

Present Indicative (1937)

⁞   ⁞   ⁞

It really is unbelievably difficult to act like a moron
when one isn't a moron.

To a child actor colleague, Michael Mac Liammoir

⁞   ⁞   ⁞

PERRY: I love *Peter Pan*.
ZELDA: That's because you've got a mother-fixation.
All sensitive lads with mother-fixations worship
Peter Pan.

Waiting in the Wings (1960)

And if it wasn't Peter, it was that other Pan fellow. He was introduced by his
childhood friend, Esmé Wynne . . .

She wrote poems. Reams and reams of them, love
songs, sonnets, and villanelles: alive with elves,
mermaids, leafy glades, and Pan (a good deal of Pan).

Present Indicative (1937)

Which duly led Noël to try his hand at a novel to be called *Cherry Pan* . . .

Cherry Pan, I regret to tell you, was the daughter of
the Great God Pan and was garrulous and tiresome
to the point of nausea. Having materialised suddenly
on a summer evening in Sussex, she proceeded with

excruciating pagan archness to wreak havoc in a
country parsonage before returning winsomely to her
woodland glades and elfin grots. I remember being
bitterly offended by a friend who suggested that the
title should be changed to *Bedpan*.

Speech at a literary lunch

:::   :::   :::

There was a loveable old professor who suddenly
inherited a family of merry little kiddos . . . We were
all jolly and mischievous in act one and then we all
went to sleep in a magic garden and became elves and
gnomes and what have you for acts two and three.
Some of us have remained fairies to this day.

George Banks in 'Me and the Girls'

As a child actor himself under the eagle eye of a 'stage mother' he had
plenty of opportunity to study the phenomenon at close quarters as audition
succeeded audition:

> *Don't put your daughter on the stage, Mrs. Worthington,*
> *Don't put your daughter on the stage,*
> *The profession is overcrowded*
> *And the struggle's pretty tough*
> *And admitting the fact*
> *She's burning to act*
> *That isn't quite enough.*

'Mrs. Worthington' (1936)

It was rarely a pretty sight and the song was his attempt to provide a corrective:

It is a genuine *cri de coeur* . . . Unhappily, its
effectiveness, from the point of view of propaganda,

has been negligible. I had hoped, by writing it, to
discourage misguided maternal ambition, to deter
those dreadful eager mothers from making beasts of
themselves, boring the hell out of me and wasting their
own and my time, but I have not succeeded . . . ninety-
nine out of a hundred of the letters they write to me
refer to it with roguish indulgence, obviously secure in
the conviction that it could not in any circumstance
apply to them. This is saddening, of course, but
realising that the road of the social reformer is paved
with disillusions I have determined to rise above it.

The Noël Coward Song Book (1953)

On seeing one of these child prodigies dominate and sink a play, despite
considerable critical acclaim, Coward remarked as he left the theatre:

Two things in that play should have been cut. The
second act and that child's throat.

Attributed

On another occasion he was less than pleased with a child actor's
performance in a musical version of *Gone With the Wind*. When an on-
stage horse performed a natural function – perhaps in a spirit of
constructive criticism – Coward observed:

If they'd stuffed the child's head up the horse's arse,
they would have solved two problems at once.

His views on what constituted good theatre were deeply held and
unchanged throughout his life. Nor did he miss many opportunities to
restate them:

The theatre must be treated with respect. It is a
house of strange enchantment, a temple of dreams.

⁙   ⁙   ⁙

What is most emphatically is *not* and never will be is a scruffy, illiterate, fumed-oak drill-hall serving as a temporary soap-box for political propaganda.

'A Warning to Actors', *Sunday Times* (1961)

⁙   ⁙   ⁙

Consider the public. Treat it with tact and courtesy. It will accept much from you if you are clever enough to win it to your side. Never fear it or despise it. Coax it, charm it, interest it, stimulate it, shock it now and then if you must, make it laugh, make it cry and make it think, but above all . . . never, never, never bore the living hell out of it.

Sunday Times (1961)

⁙   ⁙   ⁙

. . . as long as I continue to write plays to be acted in theatres, I shall strain every fibre to see that they are clear, well constructed and strong enough in content, either serious or funny, to keep an average paying audience interested from 8:30 until 11:15. Here endeth the first and last and, for me, only lesson.

Diaries (1956)

American producer, Gilbert Miller was Noël's own first mentor on the subject of what constituted a good play . . .

He said that someone had told his father (Henry Miller), who in turn had told him, that the construction of a play was as important as the foundations of a house, whereas dialogue, however good, could only, at best, be considered as interior decoration.

Present Indicative (1937)

Noël took the advice so much to heart that in later years he would preach it to others . . .

Before the first word of the first act is written, the last act should be clearly in the author's mind, if not actually written out in the form of a synopsis. Dialogue, for those who have a talent for it, is easy; but construction, with or without talent, is difficult and is of paramount importance. I know this sounds like heresy in this era of highly-praised, half-formulated moods, but no mood, however exquisite, is likely to hold the attention of an audience for two hours and a half unless it is based on a solid structure.

Future Indefinite (1954)

⁙   ⁙   ⁙

ROLAND: Plots aren't important, it's ideas that matter. Look at Chekhov.
GARRY: In addition to ideas I think we might concede Chekhov a certain flimsy sense of psychology, don't you?

Present Laughter (1939)

⁙   ⁙   ⁙

The most important ingredients of a play are life, death, food, sex and money – but not necessarily in that order.

Dick Richards, *The Wit of Noël Coward* (1968)

⁞⁞⁞   ⁞⁞⁞   ⁞⁞⁞

Your characters should say less at one go, unless it is a highly dramatic scene. *Don't* under rate your Audience so dreadfully – instead of letting your people *say* how and what they're feeling – let them express it more subtly – the Audience will get it all right.

Advice to his literary soulmate, Esmé Wynne (c. 1915)

And a pre-emptive word of warning to the current crop of gay young directors who insist on preaching the flawed gospel of what 'darling Noël *would* have done or written, if it hadn't been for that stupid censorship . . .'

Suggestion is always more interesting than statement.

⁞⁞⁞   ⁞⁞⁞   ⁞⁞⁞

HELEN: The great thing in this world is not to be obvious – over *anything*!

The Vortex (1924)

Despite his many talents, writing plays was what he did first and last and what he always came back to. It was his work:

The only way to enjoy life is to work. Work is much more fun than fun.

Observer Sayings of the Week (1963)

⁞⁞⁞   ⁞⁞⁞   ⁞⁞⁞

It seems to me that a professional writer should be animated by no other motive than the desire to write and, by doing so, to earn his living.

Introduction to Play Parade (1934)

On the nature of inspiration . . .

Ideas do not come to you through wandering around in the woods, hoping for inspiration. It just isn't there. It's in your head.

⠿   ⠿   ⠿

She felt suddenly cheerful, with that cheerfulness only writers know when they have successfully completed a morning's work.

'Bon Voyage'

⠿   ⠿   ⠿

I can see no particular virtue in writing quickly; on the contrary, I am well aware that too great a facility is often dangerous and should be curbed when it shows signs of getting the bit too firmly between its teeth. No reputable writer should permit his talent to bolt with him.

Future Indefinite (1954)

In 1956 in Jamaica he took up and took to writing verse . . .

I find it quite fascinating to write at random, sometimes in rhyme, sometimes not. I am trying to discipline myself away from too much discipline, by which I mean that my experience and training in lyric writing has made me inclined to stick too closely to a rigid form. It is strange that technical accuracy should occasionally banish magic, but it does. The carefully rhymed verses, which I find it very difficult *not* to do, are, on the whole, less effective and certainly less moving than the free ones.

Diaries (1956)

Even though anyone charged with typing what he wrote had quite a task . . .

My handwriting looks as though Chinese ants have crawled all over the paper.

To Cole Lesley – *Remembered Laughter* (1976)

⁘　⁘　⁘

I have a slight reforming urge, but I have rather cunningly kept it down.

The Times (1969)

⁘　⁘　⁘

GARRY: If you wish to be a playwright . . . go and get yourself a job as a butler in a repertory company, if they'll have you. Learn from the ground up how plays are constructed and what is actable and what isn't. Then sit down and write at least twenty plays one after the other, and if you can manage to get the twenty-first produced for a Sunday night performance you'll be damned lucky.

Present Laughter (1939)

Nonetheless, it was a *skill* that one honed in the live theatre, not the study:

> It's no use to go and take courses in playwriting any more than it's much use taking courses in acting. Better play to a bad matinée in Hull, it will teach you much more than a year of careful instruction.
>
> Television interview (1969)

In the same interview he would add:

> Come to think of it, I never did play to a *good* matinée in Hull . . .

His own start had been far from stellar. On his first visit to New York in 1921 he found no one beating a path to his rented door. Finally he was offered a fee of $500 by *Metropolitan Magazine* to adapt *I'll Leave It To You* into a short story:

> I reflected gleefully that for $500 I would gladly consider turning *War and Peace* into a music-hall sketch.
>
> *Present Indicative* (1937)

⋮   ⋮   ⋮

> Young playwrights would do well to compare their reviews with their royalty statements.
>
> Dick Richards, *The Wit of Noël Coward* (1968)

During his own period of dramatic apprenticeship Noël was in the habit of jotting down scraps of dialogue that might come in useful later on:

> She was so *embonpoint* before her marriage that her fiancé used to use her as a cake stand.

⠿   ⠿   ⠿

She fell down a lift shaft on Ascension Day – so perverse of her.

⠿   ⠿   ⠿

– As Oscar Wilde might have said, golf is essentially the massive in pursuit of the minute.
– I don't see why you should imagine the poor man would ever say anything so unfunny.

⠿   ⠿   ⠿

Sarcasm from you is reminiscent of a bevy of elephants leaping round a gadfly and imagining they're teasing it.

⠿   ⠿   ⠿

She's the kind of woman who only uses the Bible for blasphemous reference.

⠿   ⠿   ⠿

– Do you think a doctor would give a professional secret away?
– Of course not – honour among thieves.

⠿   ⠿   ⠿

Never take anything seriously, except perhaps bath salts.

⁙　　⁙　　⁙

My dear, there's nothing so ordinary as to try to be extraordinary.

⁙　　⁙　　⁙

She didn't like mustard, otherwise she was perfectly normal.

⁙　　⁙　　⁙

It was just that she had a complete set of Ella Wheeler Wilcox that prejudiced you.

⁙　　⁙　　⁙

My dear, she just missed being beautiful by buying her clothes ready-made.

⁙　　⁙　　⁙

She lives at Croydon and wants to see more of life.

From an early stage he was associated with the writing of comedies:

To me the essence of good comedy writing is that perfectly ordinary phrases such as 'Just fancy!' should, by virtue of their context, achieve greater laughs than the most literate epigrams. Some of the biggest laughs in *Hay Fever* occur on such lines as 'Go on', 'No, there isn't, is there?' and 'This haddock's disgusting'. There are many other glittering examples of my sophistication in the same vein.

Comedy is nearly always despised in its generation
and honoured more latterly – except by the public.

Dick Richards, *The Wit of Noël Coward* (1968)

He enjoyed humour that relied on the substitution of another word – often the opposite – for the original . . .

Let me be the eighth to congratulate you.

⁙　　⁙　　⁙

Poor man . . . he's completely unspoilt by failure.

⁙　　⁙　　⁙

He was an abstract painter with a very abstract talent.

⁙　　⁙　　⁙

There is less in this than meets the eye.

⁙　　⁙　　⁙

His thinking is the triumph of never mind over doesn't matter.

⁙　　⁙　　⁙

She suffered for years in a lack of concentration camp.

⁙　　⁙　　⁙

– It will bring out the colour in your eyes.
– Much better leave it where it is, then.

Cole Lesley – *Remembered Laughter* (1976)

Or the use of the ordinary in an unexpected context . . .

> RUTH: The mousse wasn't quite right.
> CHARLES: It *looked* a bit hysterical but it tasted delicious.

Blithe Spirit (1941)

When asked to admire one of Romney Marsh's dramatic sunsets . . .

> Too red. Very affected.

(To be fair, Oscar Wilde had said something very similar.)

:::   :::   :::

> LESTER: Louise was always an angel but her hats were misguided.

Long Island Sound (1947)

:::   :::   :::

> . . . her loveliness triumphed over many inopportune bows and ostrich feathers.

Describing Laurette Taylor in *Present Indicative* (1937)

:::   :::   :::

She was wearing a hat that looked like it was in a great hurry and couldn't stay around for long.

Tonight At 8:30 (1935)

:::   :::   :::

His eyes looked as though they were permanently scared of being separated from one another and seemed to be edging closer and closer together.

'Mrs. Capper's Birthday'

Her enormous bouffant hairdo diminished her sharp little face so that she resembled a marmoset wearing a busby.

'Mrs. Capper's Birthday'

⁜　⁜　⁜

She has no go in her, that girl. She borrowed the top of my Thermos, and never returned it. Shallow, very shallow.

The Young Idea (1922)

⁜　⁜　⁜

PAWNIE: Look at the furniture . . . look at that lamp-shade! . . . Too unrestrained. Such a bad example to the servants.

The Vortex (1924)

⁜　⁜　⁜

My dear, always make sure your eyebrows are properly lit. You can't play comedy without eyebrows.

To actress Patience Collier

⁜　⁜　⁜

It's so easy to get laughs and so difficult to control them. And that's the essence of comedy.

BBC Television interview, 'Great Acting' (1966)

⁘   ⁘   ⁘

CRESTWELL: Comedies of manners swiftly become obsolete when there are no longer any manners.

Relative Values (1951)

But with him the play was – first, last and always – the thing . . .

I am light-minded. I would inevitably write a comedy if – God help me! – I wanted to write a play with a message.

Diaries (1959)

Coward had no time for artistic pretension in the theatre and frequently observed that the avant-garde piece hailed by the intellectual press often failed to find comparable acclaim at the box office. This was not the route he ever intended to pursue:

I've never written for the intelligentsia. Sixteen curtain calls and closed on Saturday.

Interview with the *Daily Mirror*

⁘   ⁘   ⁘

My plays are written for the public and not for that small galaxy of scruffy critics and pretentious savants who know little and do less.

Diaries (1956)

⠿　　⠿　　⠿

I am quite prepared to admit that during my fifty-odd years of theatre-going, I have on many occasions been profoundly moved by plays about the Common Man, as in my fifty-odd years of restaurant-going I have frequently enjoyed tripe and onions, but I am not prepared to admit that an exclusive diet of either would be completely satisfying.

The Common Man, unless written or portrayed with genius, is not dramatically nearly so interesting as he is claimed to be.

'A Warning to Actors', *Sunday Times* (1961)

⠿　　⠿　　⠿

The age of the Common Man has taken over a nation which owes its very existence to uncommon men.

Diaries (1956)

⠿　　⠿　　⠿

I am becoming almighty sick of the Welfare State; sick of general 'commonness', sick of ugly voices, sick of bad manners and teenagers and debased values.

Diaries (1963)

⠿　　⠿　　⠿

It is dull to write incessantly about tramps and prostitutes as it is to write incessantly about dukes and duchesses and even suburban maters and paters, and it is bigoted and stupid to believe that tramps and prostitutes and under-privileged housewives frying onions and using ironing boards are automatically the salt of the earth and that nobody else is worth bothering about. It is true that a writer should try to hold the mirror up to nature, although there are aspects of nature that would be better unreflected.

'A Warning to Pioneers', *Sunday Times* (1961)

On the other hand, the answer was not to go to the opposite extreme of mindless froth:

I would like to prove that talent and material count for more than sequins and tits.

Referring to *Ace of Clubs* in his *Diaries* (1950)

Often the hardest part of a show was deciding what to call it. When producers Charles Russell and Lance Hamilton were looking for a name for the first of the *Night of 100 Stars* charity galas, there was a suggestion that it might be called *Summer Stars* – to which Noël quipped: 'Some are not!' On another occasion the author of a new show was debating what to call it and suggested *An Enquiry into Certain Aspects of the Dogmas of World War One* – to which Coward replied: 'Too snappy.' And when Russian-born Vernon Duke (*né* Vladimir Dukelsky) produced his first musical, *Yvonne*, Noël retitled it: *Ivan the Terrible*.

When there was some difficulty in deciding on a title for the first Coward anthology show, one of the production team suggested *Cream of Coward*. 'That would be asking for trouble,' Noël replied bleakly. Nevertheless, he orchestrated the dairy theme. At his suggestion the show was eventually called *Cowardy Custard* (1972).

And when it came to performing the plays:

I think the most dangerous theory advanced in modern days is that you have to feel what you do for eight performances a week. It's out of the question. And also, acting is not a state of being. Acting is acting . . . It's giving an impression of feeling. If it's real feeling, then you're very liable to lose your performance and lose the attention of the audience, because if you lose yourself, you're liable to lose them.

BBC Television interview, 'Great Acting' (1966)

⠿ ⠿ ⠿

Timing is 70% of acting.

Attributed

⠿ ⠿ ⠿

Writing is more important than acting, for one very good reason: it lasts. Stage acting only lives in people's memories as long as they live. Writing is creative; acting is interpretive. Only occasionally does very good acting become creative.

Sunday Telegraph (1966)

Coward was that unusual phenomenon – a playwright who also acted.

Acting is an instinct. A gift that is often given to people who are very silly as people. But as they come on to the stage, up goes the temperature.

⠿ ⠿ ⠿

I don't know what it [star quality] is, but I've got it.

Kathleen Tynan, *The Life of Kenneth Tynan* (1987)

Later – in his 1967 play of that name – he would attempt to define it . . .

DIRECTOR: . . . I leave to the last the question of talent. That's the pay-off, the definitive answer to all the silly riddles. That's their basic power, their natural gift for acting. I don't suppose a star has ever acted really badly in her life. I don't believe she could if she tried. That is her one reality, the foundation upon which the whole structure of her charm and personality rests, and, believe you me, it's rock solid. But that Star Quality is what transcends everything else. It's beyond definition and beyond praise. Whether they're born with it or how and where they manage to acquire it, I neither know nor care, but it's there all right. It's there as strongly in comedy as it is in tragedy.

You can be at a matinée in Manchester – or even in Hull. The play is lousy, the fortnight's notice is up on the board and the audience is so dull, you think half of them must be dead. That was the first act.

By the last they're sitting on the edge of their seats and at the final curtain they scream the place down. The hair rises on your scalp, the tears are cascading down your face and you solemnly bless the day that you were born.

And *that*, my friends, is Star Quality.

Much as he adored the craft of acting, he had few illusions about some of its practitioners:

> Theatrical people are notoriously facile of emotion, and frequently victimised by their own foolish sentimentality.
>
> *Present Indicative* (1937)

⁙ ⁙ ⁙

> BRIAN (THE AUTHOR): Why can't people in the theatre behave like normal human beings?
> TONY (DIRECTOR'S ASSISTANT): There wouldn't be a theatre if they did.
>
> *Star Quality* (1967)

⁙ ⁙ ⁙

> All acting worth the name is ham. We rehearse for weeks to hide it, but it's there all the time.
>
> To Marie Tempest (1934)

Advising a young actress on the need to project:

> When young I remember having a downward-looking view from the Gallery of Tree and Hawtrey and I could hear every word. But now, swathed in stardom in the stalls, I find I don't hear as well as in the old days.
>
> Dick Richards, *The Wit of Noël Coward* (1968)

⁙ ⁙ ⁙

> The actor is a recollection with a lot of gold dust on it.

Advice to his fellow actors:

> Speak clearly, don't bump into people, and if you
> must have motivation, think of your pay packet on
> Friday.
>
> Speech to the Gallery First Nighters' Club (1962)

And on the subject of stage fright . . .

> It is only natural, I think, that established stars
> should become more and more prone to stage fright
> as the years stack up behind them . . . I have little
> patience, however, with those who indulge their
> nervousness to the extent of spoiling their
> performances . . . If an actor is undisciplined enough
> to allow his own self-consciousness to intervene
> between himself and his talent, he should leave the
> theatrical profession and devote himself to some less
> agitating profession.
>
> *Past Conditional* (1965)

In *Sigh No More* (1945) an enthusiastic but inexperienced young male
dancer playing Harlequin had forgotten to wear his 'protector'. When he
had leapt about a little, Noël instructed the choreographer, Wendy Toye:

> For God's sake, go and tell that young man to take
> that Rockingham tea service out of his tights.

⁙   ⁙   ⁙

> LORRAINE (THE STAR): God preserve us from
> enthusiastic amateurs who have ghastly theories
> about acting and keep on talking about rhythm and
> colour.

BRYAN: I thought his *Hamlet* was marvellous.
LORRAINE: All that unbleached linen and kapok.
The Closet scene looked like a tea-tent.

Star Quality (1967)

⁞ ⁞ ⁞

JOANNA: I expect it's because you're an actor,
they're always apt to be a bit *papier mâché*.
GARRY: Just puppets, Joanna dear, creatures of
tinsel and sawdust, how clever of you to have
noticed it.

Present Laughter (1939)

⁞ ⁞ ⁞

Actors are incredibly silly, and leading ladies idiotic.

Diaries (1961)

Noël's put-downs of leading ladies were legendary. In the 1964 revival of *Hay Fever* when Edith Evans consistently read the line, 'You can see Marlow on a clear day, so they tell me' as '. . . on a *very* clear day', Noël corrected her with, 'No, dear, on a *very* clear day you can see Marlowe *and* Beaumont *and* Fletcher.' At a later performance she 'took her curtain calls as though she had just been un-nailed from the cross'.

In the 1956 television version of *Blithe Spirit*, Claudette Colbert ('I'd wring her neck – if I could find it') was fluffing her lines badly:

– Oh, dear, I knew them backwards this morning.
– And that's just the way you're delivering them,
dear.

Judy Campbell was on a wartime tour of the provinces with Coward. Exasperated with what she considered his temperamental behaviour, she finally snapped:

— Oh, I could just *throw* something at you!
— Try starting with my lines.

(1943)

On Gladys Cooper's inability to remember hers in *Relative Values* (1951):

I did not expect word perfection at the first rehearsal but I had rather hoped for it on the first night.

To an actress whose first-night performance was plagued with technical problems:

You managed to play the first act of my little comedy tonight with all the Chinese flair and light-hearted brilliance of Lady Macbeth.

Having seen the French actress Simone Signoret play Lady Macbeth in English for the first time, he summed up the production as:

Aimez-vous Glamis?

Washington Post (1969)

When an actress playing Queen Victoria had left Coward distinctly unamused:

I never realised before that Albert married beneath his station.

Evening Standard (1965)

⁙ ⁙ ⁙

· 30 ·

She stopped the show – but then the show wasn't really travelling very fast.

⁙   ⁙   ⁙

MAUD: I was in *Miss Mouse* at the Adelphi and I had a number in the last act called 'Don't Play the Fool with a Schoolgirl'. It used to stop the show.
CORA: So far as I can remember it was the notices that stopped the show.

Waiting in the Wings (1961)

Coward once attended a session of the Actors' Studio and heard Lee Strasberg recall Eleanor Duse:

{He} explained that when she smiled she didn't merely smile with her mouth, but with every part of her body! Which comes under the heading of the neatest trick of the week.

Diaries (1965)

But even the most eminent of theatrical *eminences grises* has to start somewhere . . .

DAME ROSIE:
My very first step
Was Shakespearean 'rep'
Where an awful old 'Ham' used to train us.
I'd nothing to do
In The Dream *and* The Shrew
But I carried a spear
In King John *and* King Lear
And a hatchet in Coriolanus.
I ranted for years

· 31 ·

In pavilions on piers
Til my spirits were really at zero,
Then I got a small role
Of a Tart with a soul
In a play by Sir Arthur Pinero.

'Three Theatrical Dames' from *Hoi Polloi* (1947)
– unproduced musical

⠿⠀⠀⠿⠀⠀⠿

Many years ago I remember a famous actress explaining to me with perfect seriousness that before making an entrance she always stood aside and let God go on first. I can also remember that on that particular occasion He gave a singularly uninspired performance.

Stage Fright (1965)

⠿⠀⠀⠿⠀⠀⠿

When I eventually write my book on the theatre there will be a whole chapter devoted to leading ladies' dresses and hair. They are invariably the main stumbling-blocks. Leading ladies' husbands may also come in for some acrid comment.

Diaries (1961)

⠿⠀⠀⠿⠀⠀⠿

Poor darling glamorous stars everywhere, their lives are so lonely and wretched and frustrated. Nothing but applause, flowers, Rolls-Royces, expensive hotel suites, constant adulation. It's too pathetic and wrings the heart.

Diaries (1955)

⠿   ⠿   ⠿

Great big glamorous stars can be very tiresome.

Diaries (1956)

⠿   ⠿   ⠿

It is sad to think how many of our glamorous leading ladies are round the bend.

Diaries (1958)

⠿   ⠿   ⠿

She got in a rage
About age
And retired, in a huff, from the stage.
Which, taken all round, was a pity
Because she was still fairly pretty
But she got in a rage
About age . . .

And she moaned and she wept and she wailed
And she roared and she ranted and railed
And retired, very heavily veiled,
From the stage.

'Epitaph for an Elderly Actress', *Collected Verse* (1984)

⠿   ⠿   ⠿

God preserve me in future from female stars. I don't suppose He will. I really am too old and tired to go through all these tired old hoops.

Diaries (1956)

But without a doubt his *leading* leading lady – both professionally and personally – was Gertrud Alexandra Dagmar Lawrence-Klausen (Gertie Lawrence). They met as fellow child actors in 1913 and Coward recorded their meeting in *Present Indicative*. She was, he recalled:

> A vivacious child with ringlets to whom I took an instant fancy . . . her face was far from pretty, but tremendously alive. She was very *mondaine*, carried a handbag with a powder-puff and frequently dabbed her generously turned-up nose. She confided to me that her name was Gertrude Lawrence, but that I was to call her Gert because everybody did.

Although the names 'Noël and Gertie' became indissolubly linked, in fact they only appeared together twice as adult actors – in *Private Lives* (1930) and *Tonight At 8:30* (1936). So popular were they with the public that they talked often of the future plays he would write for the two of them. Their relationship was based on their irreverent affection for each other. Even the

humble telegram could be turned into a medium for wit when she was the subject. On opening in her first straight play:

> LEGITIMATE AT LAST STOP WON'T
> MOTHER BE PLEASED

On a subsequent first night:

> A WARM HAND ON YOUR OPENING

And on her 1940 marriage to Richard Aldrich:

> DEAR MRS. A HOORAY HOORAY
> AT LAST YOU ARE DEFLOWERED
> ON THIS AS EVERY OTHER DAY
> I LOVE YOU NOEL COWARD

On one occasion Coward was invited to write a typical Hollywood film script to star Gertie. He replied:

> REGRET CANNOT WRITE LIFE OF SARAH
> BERNHARDT FOR GERTRUDE LAWRENCE
> STOP TOO BUSY WRITING LIFE OF
> ELEONORA DUSE FOR BEATRICE LILLIE

(Or in some versions – 'St Teresa for Mae West')

But even affection was not allowed to stand in the way of professional perfectionism. Miss Lawrence was known to sing famously flat on occasion . . .

> If you would sing a little *more* out of tune, darling, you would find yourself singing in thirds, which would be a *great* improvement.
>
> *Noël Coward Song Book* (1953)

Coward was as objective about his own stage persona as he was about other people's. Asked in a television interview if he had ever been the subject of a 'put-down', he replied:

> Yes, I once left a stage door and there was a glamorous crowd welcoming me with autograph books, which I was graciously signing, when I heard someone say – 'I'll swap you three Noël Cowards for one Jessie Matthews'.

Had he ever told Miss Matthews?

> Yes, she didn't speak to me for three weeks, she was so pleased with herself.

> Television interview (1968)

As an actor, he was well aware of his range and the need to stay within it. Shakespeare intrigued him, and many of his plays took their titles from Shakespearean quotations – *Blithe Spirit, Present Laughter, This Happy Breed* - but to *act* the Bard was quite another matter:

> I was offered Hamlet five times . . . I just knew that the day I declaimed 'To be or not to be' in public, it would be the death of me.

> *Daily Mail* (1969)

Would he contemplate it in the future?

> I think I've left it a bit late! I might play the Nurse in *Romeo and Juliet*.

He also thought he might be 'rather good as Madame Arcati'!

Having played King Magnus in Shaw's *The Apple Cart* during Coronation Year . . .

> I am not at all certain that in the future when I write a part I shall not write myself a king; it really is so satisfactory to have all the other characters standing up so often.
>
> *Diaries* (1953)

There was a fair amount of Noël Coward in Garry Essendine – with a welcome splash of self-deprecation . . .

> GARRY: I'm always acting – watching myself go by – that's what's so horrible – I see myself all the time eating, drinking, loving, suffering . . . my life is not my own . . . I belong to the public and to my work.
>
> *Present Laughter* (1939)

To Rattigan after lukewarm reception for *The Sleeping Prince* . . .

> Don't worry, Terence, I not only fuck up some of my plays by writing them but I frequently fuck them up by acting in them as well.

And Coward was perfectly realistic about his relative stature as an actor . . .

> If you were to put me on a stage with Laurence Olivier, John Gielgud and Ralph Richardson, they would be acting me off the stage and out of the auditorium – but everyone in the audience would be looking at me.
>
> To his godson, Daniel Massey (attributed)

Although many considered him the definitive performer of his own songs, the verdict was not unanimous. A critic reviewing his 1951 cabaret début at the Café de Paris accused him of 'massacring' his material. If so, Coward declared in his *Diaries*:

> It was the most profitable massacre since the St. Valentine's Day massacre.

Nonetheless, he had no illusions about his technical vocal accomplishments:

> It is a composer's voice. It has considerable range but no tone, little music, but lots of meaning.

⁞   ⁞   ⁞

> I can't sing but I know how to, which is quite different.
>
> *Observer* (1969)

Cabaret in London and Las Vegas was to lead to television, but the technical aspects of this new miracle medium, of course, were quite beyond him . . .

> . . . my brain shudders at the very idea.
>
> *Future Indefinite* (1954)

As early as 1947 he was inclined to dismiss the new medium . . .

> What I have learned so far is that, apart from a few special personalities and talents, the standard of entertainment is poor, the lighting unpredictable, and the commercial emphasis very overstressed. I have seen to date few evidences of imagination in production and no sense of experimentation.
>
> *Diaries* (1955)

. . . but when he found himself having to tackle it professionally, he discovered all it needed was his usual discipline . . .

> The TV spectacular I am going to do with Mary Martin will be completely spontaneous. The kind of spontaneity I like best – the kind that comes after five weeks' rehearsal.

> (1955)

In that same year he was forced to admit that 'this curious medium' had its artistic advantages – even for a middle-aged playwright:

> The cutting of my plays down for television is certainly a salutary experience, and I believe that the next time I embark on a full-length play for the theatre, I shall find that I have profited by it. I shall have learned, for instance, to dispense with amusing irrelevancies that have no direct bearing on the story and to get back to my original method of saying what I have to say in as few lines as possible with a minimum of atmospheric padding and linguistic flourishes.

> *Diaries* (1956)

Coward had a career-long feud with dramatic critics. Having received virtually unqualified praise in his early twenties, he found himself an early victim of media 'deconstruction' for much of the rest of his life. His crusade of retaliation didn't help matters:

> Criticism and Bolshevism have one thing in common. They both seek to pull down that which they could never build.

> (1925)

⁜   ⁜   ⁜

I have always been fond of them [critics] . . . I think it is so frightfully clever of them to go night after night to the theatre and know so little about it.

⁛   ⁛   ⁛

I don't know what makes them so vitriolic; I suppose it's my continued success and something about my personality that infuriates them, in which case I fear they will have to get on with it.

Diaries (1959)

⁛   ⁛   ⁛

Alas, in public life it is often necessary to take the rough with the smooth, and occasionally with the rough.

'A Richer Dust'

⁛   ⁛   ⁛

If I had really cared about the critics, I would have shot myself in the Twenties.

Play Parade Volume 4 (1954)

⁛   ⁛   ⁛

I can take any amount of criticism, so long as it is unqualified praise.

Press interview

⁛   ⁛   ⁛

'I have a great friend who is a journalist,' I said.
'She's a darling.'

'Then she must be a very bad journalist,' snapped
Buddha. 'No good journalist could go on being a
darling even if she started as one.'

Pomp and Circumstance (1960)

⁂   ⁂   ⁂

Newspaper reporting, either of events or people,
depends for its effectiveness on superficial
observation and snap judgements; speed and brevity
are essential and there is rarely time for subtle
analysis or true assessment of character. Usually, in
the case of a celebrity, the label has been fixed and
the clichés set for years.

(1952)

⁂   ⁂   ⁂

The critics described *Private Lives* variously as
'tenuous, thin, brittle, gossamer, iridescent and
delightfully daring'. All of which connoted in the
public mind cocktails, repartee and irreverent allusions
to copulation, thereby causing a gratifying number of
respectable people to queue up at the box office.

Play Parade Volume 1 (1934)

Even so, it would be hypocritical to pretend that good reviews did not stroke
a writer's feathers the right way. Certainly they did for Evan Lorrimer,
Noël's novelist in 'What Mad Pursuit?'

Such allusions . . . are immensely agreeable.
Unimportant, perhaps, in their essence, but in their

implication very important indeed. Just as millions of little coral animals in so many years construct a barrier reef against the sea, so can these small accolades, over a period of time, build, if not quite a barrier reef, at least a fortification against the waves of oblivion.

But Coward remained philosophical:

> For who is to say with any certainty which of an
> artist's works are his best? Everyone knows that
> contemporary judgment is not to be relied upon and
> in fact it is a fairly safe rule to take the opposite view
> to the current one. Even Time will not tell, for an
> artist is sometimes remembered and loved for his
> more popular works rather than his best . . .
>
> Magazine interview (1939)

And throughout his career he remained ruthlessly *self*-critical . . .

> I seem in later years to have lost my gift for economy.
>
> *Diaries* (1955)

The last show that Coward ever saw was a gala performance of the New
York compilation revue *Oh, Coward!* Asked if he was laughing at the lines,
he replied:

> One doesn't laugh at his own jokes.
>
> (1973)

But perhaps the line that best sums up Coward on theatre was this one:

> If you're a star, you should behave like one. I always
> have.
>
> *Sunday Times* (1969)

PART TWO

::: ::: :::

'A Marvellous Party'

The English class system was a recurrent theme in Coward's work. Although his own origins were lower-middle class, the public persona he created enabled him to mingle with all levels of society.

> The cream of the aristocracy mingles with the clotted cream of the (theatrical) profession.
>
> Introduction to Three Plays

⁙   ⁙   ⁙

> I think social distinctions are very important because they make a balance.
>
> Interview with Edgar Lustgarten (1972)

And he added somewhat defensively:

> If I were only interested in the Ritz and Royalty could I have written *Brief Encounter* and *This Happy Breed*?

His perception ensured that he saw all of its strata clearly and took none of them entirely seriously. There was the Landed Gentry:

> *The Stately Homes of England,*
> *How beautiful they stand,*
> *To prove the upper classes*
> *Have still the upper hand;*

Though the fact that they have to be rebuilt
And frequently mortgaged to the hilt
Is inclined to take the gilt
Off the gingerbread . . .

'The Stately Homes of England' – *Operette* (1938)

⁖　　⁖　　⁖

AMANDA: Whose yacht is that?
ELYOT: The Duke of Westminster's I expect. It always is.

Private Lives (1936)

But there was aristocracy and aristocracy. Observing a mixed bag of minor honourables at a society wedding long after the Royals had departed, Coward remarked to a fellow guest, Richard Burton:

Here come the riff-raff.

And then, of course, there were the Poor Rich . . . Considering his friends, the Westminsters:

Stone walls do not a prison make nor iron bars a cage, but millions of pounds can make, very subtly, both.

(1962)

During his lifetime, Coward's beady eye was always busy 'watching Society scampering past' and observing its mores shift. In the 1920s it was perfectly permissible – even de rigeur – to appear socially frivolous:

EUSTACE: The only thing more expensive than hunting is virtue.

The Young Idea (1921)

⁙   ⁙   ⁙

CICELY: I do wish you wouldn't despise my husband
so, Roddy, it isn't good form.

The Young Idea (1921)

⁙   ⁙   ⁙

JENNIFER: I have never been able to take anything
seriously after eleven o'clock in the morning.

The Young Idea (1921)

⁙   ⁙   ⁙

If it's rissoles, I shan't dress – a rule I made in 1929
and to which I still strictly adhere.

(1956)

And the world could safely be populated with social butterflies and chinless
wonders – a species that could still be occasionally sighted years later.
Coward recalled meeting 'a startled young man fresh from Oxford with
over-eager teeth' as late as 1953 (*Diaries*).

The war, though, had changed all that and the values of the post-war
world were not particularly to Coward's liking:

FELICITY: One of the worst aspects of modern
English life is that so many of one's friends have to
work and they're so bad at it.

Relative Values (1951)

⁙   ⁙   ⁙

CRESTWELL (THE BUTLER): Above all I drink to the final inglorious disintegration of the most unlikely dream that ever troubled the foolish heart of man – Social Equality!

Relative Values (1951)

After all, weren't we *all* the Bourgeoisie now . . . ?

Long live the Bourgeoisie!
We oil our bats
And we clean our clubs,
We're democrats
In the local pubs.
We like Britannia to rule
*   the waves*
We don't believe that the
*   waves are ruled by*
*   slaves.*
Let the 'Workers' unite,
Let the classes fight
We'll be glad to referee
(From our seat on the
*   sidelines)*
Esprit de corps, lads
Wins every war, lads.
Long live the Bourgeoisie!

'Long Live the Bourgeoisie!'
from *Hoi Polloi* (1947)
– unproduced musical

There were – or should be – certain fixed points even in a changing world and over the years Coward would seek to define them:

> Class was class and there was no getting away from it.
>
> 'The Kindness of Mrs. Radcliffe'

:::   :::   :::

> EVAN: Manners are the outward expression of expert interior decoration.
>
> *Long Island Sound* (1947)

On taste:

> It can be vulgar, but it must never be embarrassing.
>
> John Lahr, *Coward the Playwright* (1982)

:::   :::   :::

> Style in everything demands discipline.
>
> *Daily Mail* (1966)

In retrospect he had to admit that his own sense of style had not always been completely impeccable . . .

> My own audition apparel was usually a navy blue suit with a coloured shirt, tie, socks, and handkerchief to match. I had not learned then that an exact duplication of colours ill becomes the well-dressed man.
>
> *Present Indicative* (1937)

In the 1950s Noël made one of his rare appearances in an advertisement. The Gillette Company, launching their new 'Aristocrat' razor blade, asked him to define 'Style'. His quirkish reply was . . .

A candy-striped jeep

Jane Austen

Cassius Clay

THE TIMES before it changed

Danny LaRue

Charleston, South Carolina

'Monsieur' de Givenchy

A zebra (but NOT a zebra crossing)

Evading boredom

Gertrude Lawrence

The Paris Opera House

White

A seagull

A Brixham trawler

Margot Fonteyn

Any Cole Porter song

English pageantry

Marlene's voice

Lingfield has a *tiny* bit

⠿　　⠿　　⠿

Conceit is an outward manifestation of inferiority.

The Times (1969)

⠿　　⠿　　⠿

I absolutely loathe champagne. Have since I was twenty.

New York Herald Tribune
(1963)

⁝   ⁝   ⁝

I've got to go out and be social,
I've got to be bright
And extremely polite
And refrain from becoming too loose or too tight
And I mustn't impose conversational blight
On the dolt on my left
And the fool on my right.
I must really be very attractive tonight
As I have to go out and be social.

Unpublished verse

When you come right down to it, he concluded quite early, each of us had to decide who we wanted to be and then set about creating that persona. He certainly devoted his own life to doing so:

LEO: It's all a question of masks, really; brittle, painted masks. We all wear them as a form of protection; modern life forces us to. We must have some means of shielding our timid, shrinking souls from the glare of civilisation.

Design For Living (1932)

Of course, for the true Social Animal, a certain amount of civilised glare was inevitable. After all, there were the inevitable parties to go to . . . and one in particular. Coward never forgot the 1930s party in the south of France to which hostess Elsa Maxwell invited him. When he arrived, he found that he was expected to entertain the guests. He firmly declined, then enshrined the occasion in song:

> *I went to a marvellous party,*
> *We played the most wonderful game,*
> *Maureen disappeared*
> *And came back in a beard*
> *And we all had to guess her name!*
> *We talked about growing old gracefully*
> *And Elsie who's seventy-four*
> *Said, 'A, it's a question of being sincere,*
> *And B, if you're supple you've nothing to fear'.*
> *Then she swung upside down from a glass chandelier,*
> *I couldn't have liked it more.*

'I Went to a Marvellous Party'
from *Set to Music* (1939)

And as the cocktails flowed at every social occasion worth the name, the talk would inevitably turn to the Arts. No matter what the year, there was the endless debate over the modern novel:

MRS. ASTON-HOOPER: I get so tired of the usual modern novels. They nearly always end with the hero having been married forty years to the heroine, gazing down the vista of his life and saying – 'I wonder', until a dotted line cuts his rather aimless musings short.

The Unattainable (1918) – unpublished play

Whatever he chose to say in his plays, in private life he was positively puritanical:

> If there's anything I hate in modern novels it is this sex obsession, this pseudo-tough realism in which every sexual depravity is intimately dissected. It drags one straight back to Jane Austen.
>
> Interview (1968)

:::   :::   :::

> It was sheer pornography. The heroine was a lesbian and a drunkard – but she finished up a nun, which was meant to mean, I suppose, that she was really all right. There was one tremendous chapter that was nothing but filth: it made me think of the dedication – 'To my dear wife, Lillian, without whom this book would not have been possible.'

He firmly believed that the sexiest book ever written was *Madame Bovary*, since it proved you could achieve any erotic effect you wished without having to resort to four letter words. And he had strong views on what he read and those who wrote it. Of Henry James – ('the King of exquisitely phrased verbosity') – more in sorrow than in anger:

> . . . poor Mr. James who trudges and writhes and wriggles through jungles of verbiage to describe a cucumber sandwich.
>
> *Diaries* (1957)

Then, of course, there was the inevitable Oscar Wilde. In the early 1950s, Noël had found the task of turning *Lady Windermere's Fan* into *After The Ball* a more difficult assignment than he had bargained for. Both men were great and original wits but their sensibilities were very different. What one liked the other loathed. As a colleague of Coward's put it – it was like having two celebrities at the same dinner party, competing for attention. Some years later the Coward mind was firmly made up:

> It is extraordinary indeed that such a posing, artificial old queen should have written one of the greatest comedies in the English language. In my opinion it was the only thing of the least *importance* that he did write.
>
> *Diaries* (1962)

In 1961 Noël wrote a series of articles for the *Sunday Times*, castigating, among others, the currently fashionable 'Kitchen Sink' playwrights. Not surprisingly, since his own reputation was in decline at the time, his motives were questioned. Nonetheless, they were views he has held consistently for some time.

Of John Osborne:

> I cannot believe that this writer, the first of the 'angry young men', was ever really angry at all. Dissatisfied, perhaps, and certainly envious and, to a degree, talented, but no more than that. No leader of thought and ideas, a conceited, calculating young man blowing a little trumpet.
>
> *Diaries* (1959)

One of the contemporary writers he did admire was Peter Shaffer, who had just written *The Royal Hunt of the Sun*:

> The difference between Peter Shaffer and all the Osbornes and Weskers is that he has no hatred in his heart and no partisan axe to grind. He writes compassionately about human beings. He also has more than a touch of poetry. I only wish he would write more.
>
> *Diaries* (1964)

After hating the early work Noël became a convert to Harold Pinter . . .

I think I'm now on Pinter's wavelength. He is at least a genuine original. I don't think he could write in any other way if he tried. *The Caretaker*, on the face of it, is everything I hate most in the theatre; squalor, repetition, lack of action, but somehow it seizes hold of you . . . Nothing happens except that somehow it does.

He had mixed views of American playwright, Edward Albee. Having found *Who's Afraid of Virginia Woolf?* (1963) 'fine, scathing, sublimely acted', he found *Tiny Alice* (1965) 'so nearly good and yet so maddeningly pretentious' and wrote to the playwright a few days later from Jamaica to clarify his reaction . . .

I have a profound respect for your rich talent . . . Expert use of language is to me a perpetual joy. You use it expertly, all right, but I fear, too self-indulgently. Your duty to me as a playgoer and a reader is to explain whatever truths you are dealing with as lucidly and accurately. I refuse to be fobbed off with a sort of metaphysical. 'What's My Line?' Let me hear from you. An ordinary love letter will do!

Letter (1965)

Years before, he had failed to fully appreciate Arthur Miller. After a performance of *Death of a Salesman* he heard someone gush that what they had just seen was not a play but an 'experience' . . .

I wish it had been a play.

Then there was art – both ancient, as on seeing the Venus de Milo:

> It's only what's to be expected if you will go on biting your nails.

Attributed

. . . and modern (a particular Coward *bête noire*):

> SEBASTIEN: I don't think anyone knows about painting any more. Art, like human nature, has got out of hand.

Nude With Violin (1954)

After reading Wilenski's book *Lives of the Impressionists:*

> Really no burlesque however extravagant could equal the phrases he uses to describe the 'Abstract' boys. Quite a lot of it is completely unintelligible. He talks a great deal of 'emotive force' and 'lyrical colour' and 'constant functional forms', etc., and after he has described a picture in approximately these terms you turn to a coloured plate and look at a square lady with three breasts and a guitar up her crotch.

Diaries (1954)

⁑   ⁑   ⁑

He's running a temperature and his chest looks like a bad Matisse.

Pomp and Circumstance (1960)

⁑   ⁑   ⁑

Perhaps I was frightened by a Bellini Madonna when I was a tiny child.

Present Indicative (1937)

Wagner and his works crop up frequently in Coward's critical litany ('Not a *tremendous* Wagnerian on account of getting fidgety' . . . 'I wish he'd get on with it') and *Parsifal* came in for particular scrutiny. Having seen *Camelot* (1955):

It's about as long as *Parsifal* and not as funny.

⁙   ⁙   ⁙

ELENA: My husband was an operatic tenor. He sang very loudly, particularly in *Norma*. I think that was what finished him.

Pacific 1860 (1946)

⁙   ⁙   ⁙

GILDA: People are wrong when they say that the opera isn't what it used to be. It *is* what it used to be – that's what's wrong with it.

Design For Living (1932)

Nor did eighteenth-century music appeal. Take Mozart . . .

All too often it sounds like a Pekinese peeing on a mink rug.

Quoted by Julian Slade

⁙   ⁙   ⁙

I don't like good music . . . I can't bear Mozart. I know I'm missing a lot, but that can't be helped.

Nor did many composers fare much better . . .

Though Wolfgang Mozart wrote The Magic Flute he
Alas, alas composed Cosi Fan Tutte . . .
But then poor Donizetti
Was likewise not
Too hot
At choosing libretti.
Then there are those Rosenkavaliers and Fledermauses
Written by all those Strausses
Which play to crowded houses
And, to me, are louses.

'Opera Notes', *Collected Verse* (1984)

⁙   ⁙   ⁙

B: She doesn't really mind what it is. She's perfectly
   happy so long as she can let her emeralds glitter to
   Chopin.
A: I've never heard Chopin there. They nearly
   always play Brahms with woebegone faces and
   India-rubber collars.

The Unattainable (1918) – unpublished play

⁙   ⁙   ⁙

STELLA: I always had my suspicions about Derek.
   There was something in the way he played the
   piano.
JUDY: Come now, Stella. He did at least play the
   piano beautifully.
STELLA: Too much Debussy.

Age Cannot Wither (1967) – unproduced play

⁙   ⁙   ⁙

Having been deafened by Wagnerian bassoons
I much prefer these ultra-British
Rather skittish
Little tunes.

'The Girl Who Came to Supper' (1963) – unpublished song

⁙   ⁙   ⁙

There has never yet been composed a piece of
classical music that was not too long.

Diaries (1964)

His own musical taste ran more to the romantic and melodic. ('I love Verdi and Donizetti and all those boys') which did not stop him tweaking them when the fancy took him . . .

> *I think we must face the fact*
> *That Carmen by Bizet*
> *Is no more Spanish than the Champs Elysées*

And . . .

> *We must admit that every hurdy-gurdy*
> *Owes a deep debt of gratitude*
> *To Giuseppe Verdi*
>
> 'Not Yet the Dodo'

Coward enjoyed the arts, and the associated 'high society' lifestyle. But he couldn't always keep up with the changing scene. After the initial sense of loss, he was inclined to wonder whether, after all, nostalgia was quite what it used to be:

> It was a *nostalgie du temps perdu* and I wasn't somehow all that sorry when the *temps* were *perdu*.
>
> *Diaries* (1966)

PART THREE

::: ::: :::

'Mad Dogs and Englishmen'

To the end of his days Coward remained a flag-waving patriot, even if the England he celebrated had become largely a figment of his memory. In many ways he was a Victorian stranded in another era and suffering from a malaise he would term 'Twentieth Century Blues':

> In this strange
>   illusion,
> Chaos and confusion,
> People seem to lose their
>   way.
> What is there to strive for,
> Love or keep alive for? Say –
> Hey, hey, call it a day.
> Blues, nothing to win or to lose.
> It's getting me down.
> Blues, I've got those weary
> Twentieth Century Blues.

> 'Twentieth Century Blues' from
> *Cavalcade* (1931)

Personally he needed to believe that the Old Country could find a new purpose. In *Cavalcade* he has the heroine (Jane Marryot), towards the end of a long life, give the New Year Toast to the Future that she has given every year:

JANE: Let's drink to the hope that one day this country of ours, which we love so much, will find dignity and greatness and peace again.

During the 1930s he came to despise Neville Chamberlain and all those who trusted the theory of appeasement. Frank Gibbons addresses his infant grandson at the end of *This Happy Breed* (1939):

You belong to a race that's been bossy for years and the reason it's held on as long as it has is that nine times out of ten it's behaved decently and treated people right. Just lately, I'll admit, we've been giving at the knees a bit and letting people down who trusted us and allowing noisy little men to bully us with a lot of guns and bombs and aeroplanes. But don't worry – that won't last – the people themselves, the ordinary people like you and me, know something better than all the fussy old politicians put together – we know what we belong to, where we come from, and where we're going. We may not know it in our brains, but we know it in our roots. And we know another thing, too, and it's this. We 'aven't lived and died and struggled all these hundreds of years to get decency and justice and freedom for ourselves without being prepared to fight fifty wars if need be – to keep 'em.

⁙   ⁙   ⁙

To most people this war has been an absolute blessing. It's not only provided them with an all-absorbing topic of conversation but furnished their empty minds with frequent opportunities for indulging in maudlin sentiment and cheap patriotism.

⁙   ⁙   ⁙

She was too interested in women's suffrage . . . and
when war broke out and there was nothing more
exciting for women to fight for than margarine – the
shock killed her!

But, on occasion, overt emotion from the supposedly cynical Mr Coward
raised a number of eyebrows and questions about his sincerity – a situation
he had aggravated by his first-night speech:

'. . . in spite of the troublous times we are living in, it
is still pretty exciting to be English' . . . quite true,
quite sincere; I felt it strongly, but I rather wished I
hadn't said it, hadn't popped it on to the top of
Cavalcade like a paper-cap.

⋮   ⋮   ⋮

The rumour was fairly general that I had written it
with my tongue in my cheek, probably in bed,
wearing a silk dressing-gown and shaking with
cynical laughter.

Present Indicative (1937)

With the arrival of the Second World War it became Noël's ambition to
write the definitive war song – something that would match Ivor Novello's
'Keep The Home Fires Burning' from the first 'war to end wars'. One
morning in 1941, sitting in a bomb-damaged London railway station after
a particularly bad blitz, the sight of a small wild flower bravely struggling
to survive seemed to symbolise something about the city and the people he
loved so much:

London Pride has been handed down to us.
London Pride is a flower that's free.
London Pride means our own dear town to us,

And our pride it forever will be . . .
Cockney feet
Mark the beat of history.
Every street
Pins a memory down.
Nothing ever can quite replace
The grace of London Town.

'London Pride' (1941)

It was a sentiment he was to express in words (and often music) for the next thirty years:

I was a flagrant, unabashed sentimentalist and likely to remain so until the end of my days. I did love England and all it stood for. I loved its follies and apathies and curious streaks of genius; I loved standing to attention for 'God Save the King'; I loved British courage, British humour, and British understatement . . . I loved the people – the ordinary, the extraordinary, the good, the bad, the indifferent, and what is more I belonged to that exasperating, weather-sodden little island with its uninspired cooking, its muddled thinking and its unregenerate pride, and it belonged to me, whether it liked it or not.

Future Indefinite (1954)

⁂   ⁂   ⁂

I *am* England and England is me.

Sunday Express (1965)

He most certainly did like it, even though he had always seen it warts and all. Even in his own early twenties he had catalogued what he saw as a dangerous *ennui* of the post-war younger generation that was knock, knock, knocking at the door . . .

> *In lives of leisure*
> *The craze for pleasure*
> *Steadily grows.*
> *Cocktails and laughter*
> *But what comes after?*
> *Nobody knows.*
>
> 'Poor Little Rich Girl' from *On With the Dance* (1925)

:::   :::   :::

> *No more the moon*
> *On the still Lagoon*
> *Can please the young enchanted,*
> *They must have this*
> *And they must have that*
> *And they take it all for granted.*
> *They hitch their star*
> *To a cocktail bar*
> *Which is all they really wanted . . .*
>
> 'The Lido Beach' from *This Year of Grace!* (1928)

One thing never disappointed – the charm of London Town . . .

> *London – is a little bit of all right,*
> *Nobody can deny that's true . . .*
> *London – is a place where you can call right*
> *Round and have a cosy cup of tea,*
> *If you're fed right up and got your tail right down*

London town
Is a wonderful place to be.

From *The Girl Who Came To Supper* (1963)

Perhaps, though, there were one or two small improvements we could make:

We downtrodden British must learn to be skittish
And give an impression of devil-may-care . . .

'Don't Make Fun of the Fair' (1951)

:::   :::   :::

We British are a peculiar breed
Undemonstrative on the whole.
It takes a very big shock indeed
To dent our maddening self-control . . .

Our far-flung Empire imposed new rules
And lasted a century or so
Until, engrossed with our football pools
We shrugged our shoulders and let it go.

'Not Yet the Dodo' (1967)

:::   :::   :::

LAURA: Do you know, I believe we should all behave quite differently if we lived in a warm, sunny climate all the time. We shouldn't be so withdrawn and shy and difficult.

Brief Encounter (1945)

As the years went by, though, he found it progressively harder to equate 'swinging sixties' England with the *Great* Britain he had known. But as late as 1957 and well after Suez he could still say:

The British Empire was a great and wonderful social, economic and even spiritual experiment, and all the parlour pinks and eager, ill-informed intellectuals cannot convince me to the contrary . . . At the present moment England is in a state of almost complete subservience to America and for the worst possible reason, that America is the richer. I, who genuinely love America and Americans, cannot ignore their only too obvious naivety in world diplomacy.

Diaries (1957)

In 1963 he attended the annual Battle of Britain dinner and found himself asking:

What was it that I so minded about twenty-three years ago? An ideal? An abstract patriotism? What? . . . I wanted suddenly to stand up and shout . . . 'Let's face the truth. The England we knew and loved was betrayed at Munich, revived for one short year in 1940 and was supreme in adversity, and now no longer exists.' That last great war was our valediction. It will never happen again.

Diaries (1963)

⁙   ⁙   ⁙

An Englishman is the highest example of a human being who is a free man.

Interview with Hunter Davies (1969)

⁜   ⁜   ⁜

I continue to tell foreigners how great we are. Before I die, I would like once again to be able to believe this myself.

Sunday Express (1965)

He was, by his own admission, 'a cosy Royal snob' and became close and genuine friends with several members of the Royal Family. When Graham Payn thanked the Queen Mother for attending Noël's memorial service in Westminster Abbey in 1984, she replied simply: 'He was my friend.' Noël liked nothing better than the 'theatre' of Royalty – the marching military bands, the salutes, the flags waving . . .

> *Everyone in London likes a damn good show,*
> *A properly planned procession or parade.*
> *It's not because we're snobs*
> *But we like to be sure the Nobs*
> *With all that kow-towing*
> *And bobbing and bowing*
> *Are bloody well doing their jobs.*
> *Flags against the sky.*
> *Horses galloping by,*
> *Yards and yards of Guards*
> *In their golden braid.*
> *We'll stand in the sun,*
> *We'll stand in the rain*
> *Or fog or sleet or snow,*
> *For Londoners like a damn good show.*

'Damn Good Show'
from *Hoi Polloi* (1947)
– unproduced musical

⁜   ⁜   ⁜

There is little sense in having a constitutional
monarchy and not being a cosy royal snob.

Diaries (1957)

Patriotic to the last, Coward loved both England and the English:

It merely occurred to me that I belonged to a most
remarkable race. In later years I have seen no reason

to revise this opinion. I am quite aware of our shortcomings, perhaps even more so than more impartial observers because I have suffered from them personally. . . However, so much as I may loathe this and that and the other, it is what I love that really counts, and what I love about my country is really quite simple. I love its basic integrity, an integrity formed over hundreds of years by indigenous humour, courage and common-sense.

Past Conditional (1965)

PART FOUR

⁛ ⁛ ⁛

'Sail Away'

We British are an island race,
The sea lies all around us,
And visitors from other lands,
With different sets of different glands,
Bewilder and astound us.

Conversation Piece (1934)

Along with his strong sense of patriotism, Noël sometimes displayed a suspicion, even a dislike, of those from other countries. To start with, there was our age-old sparring partner across the Channel:

There's always something fishy about the French!
We've a sinister suspicion
That behind their savoir-faire
They share
A common contempt
For every mother's son of us.
Tho' they smile and smirk
We know they're out for dirty work . . .
Every wise and thoroughly worldly wench
Knows there's always something fishy about the French!

Conversation Piece (1934)

Although we may not be entirely blameless ourselves:

Foreigners' immorality may make us look askance,
Though we are not above it if we get the slightest chance.
What is it makes an Englishman enjoy himself in France?

Or, if you looked across that other stretch of sea:

> The Irish behave exactly as they
> have been portrayed as behaving
> for years. Charming, soft-voiced,
> quarrelsome, Priest-ridden,
> feckless and happily devoid of the
> slightest integrity in our stodgy
> English sense of the word.
>
> On his first visit to Dublin (1960)

Then, of course, there were the Germans. Coward's side-swipe at them early in the war was totally misread by many and censored for a while until the irony was firmly established. An exception was Winston Churchill who 'liked it so much that I had to sing it to him seven times in one evening'.

> *Don't let's be beastly to the*
> *Germans*
> *When the age of peace and plenty*
> *has begun.*
> *We must send them steel and oil and coal and everything*
> *they need*
> *For their peaceable intentions can be always guaranteed.*
> *Let's employ with them a sort of 'strength through joy'*
> *with them,*
> *They're better than us at honest manly fun.*
> *Let's let them feel they're swell again and bomb us all to*
> *hell again,*
> *But don't let's be beastly to the Hun.*
>
> 'Don't Let's Be Beastly to the Germans' (1943)

⁛   ⁛   ⁛

The Germans have been aggressive, cruel and humourless all through their dismal history, and I find it quite impossible to forgive them, however politic it may be considered to do so. They are a horrid, neurotic race and always have been and always will be and, to my mind, none of their contributions to science, literature and music compensates for their turgid emotionalism and unparalleled capacity for torturing their fellow creatures.

Diaries (1955)

The Austrians, on the other hand, he always found to be 'sweet people but overmusical':

> *When we wake in the morning, the very first thing*
> *That we Austrians do is to sing and to sing.*
> *Tho' on every occasion our voices excel*
> *In a National crisis we yodel as well.*

Operette (1938)

⁙   ⁙   ⁙

ISOBEL: When she was seventeen she was sent to Geneva to be finished.

CHERRY-MAY: I should think Geneva'd be enough to finish anybody.

Nude With Violin (1956)

Yet Switzerland was a country that seemed to appeal to him from the first. In early 1939 he visited Lausanne and spent a happy time 'on the bonny, bonny banks of Lac Leman' on which he observed there was 'no lack *des cygnes*'. And in 1968 he could add . . .

I now live in Switzerland where I have a spectacular view overlooking an absolutely ravishing tax advantage.

Sunday Times

Then there were the Russians, whom he first met *in situ* in 1939 . . .

I know it is an accepted theory that the English take their pleasures sadly, but as far as I could see the Soviets didn't seem to take them at all, or perhaps there weren't any to take.

Future Indefinite (1954)

Despite his reservations, he saw earlier than most of his countrymen the sense of a single European entity – even though he cloaked his comment in a jibe . . .

I hoped we *would* go into the Common Market for the simple but valid reason that Beaverbrook was so dead against it. This I have always found a fairly safe hoe to furrow, or is it furrow to hoe?

Diaries (1963)

Most other parts of the world, it seems, he could take or leave:

> Saint Petersburg, of course, has flair
> But can be dull without the snow,
> Berlin is much too polyglot
> And Rome in summer is dreadfully hot,
> Vienna makes one ill at ease
> With those vocal Viennese,
> And Athens with its ruins and fleas
> Is far too Greek.

After the Ball (1954)

⁛   ⁛   ⁛

LEO: I've never been able to understand why the
   Japanese are such a cheerful race. All that hissing
   and grinning on the brink of destruction.
OTTO: The Japanese don't mind destruction a bit;
   they like it, it's part of their upbringing. They're
   delighted with death. Look at the way they kill
   themselves on the most whimsical of pretexts.
LEO: I always thought Madame Butterfly was over-
   hasty.

Design For Living (1932)

⁛   ⁛   ⁛

JUDY: Italians are naturally cruel, I'm afraid. Look
   how they whack away at those wretched donkeys in
   Capri.

Age Cannot Wither (1967) – unproduced play

⁛   ⁛   ⁛

*She said, 'They're just high-spirited, like all Italians
are. And most of them have a great deal more to offer
than Papa'.*

'A Bar on the Piccola Marina' (1954)

⁛   ⁛   ⁛

AMANDA: I know what the Hungarians are, too.
ELYOT: What are they?
AMANDA: Very wistful. It's all those pretzels, I
   shouldn't wonder.

Private Lives (1930)

⁞   ⁞   ⁞

SHOLTO: There's always a political crisis in Bulgaria, the same as there's always haggis in Scotland. It's traditional.

The Young Idea (1921)

In New Zealand he attended a Maori ceremony . . .

I was presented to the chiefs and the local belles, with whom I rubbed noses; this was damp but convivial. Then came the entertainment, which consisted of native songs and dances, slightly spoiled for me by the fact that the male dancers wore ordinary grey flannel trousers under their straw skirts, which, I thought, vitiated the primitive barbarity of the occasion.

Future Indefinite (1954)

⁞   ⁞   ⁞

They all insist that
South America's exotic
Whereas it couldn't be more boring
if it tried.

'Nina' (1945)

⁞   ⁞   ⁞

The one place that fascinated and frustrated him in equal measure from his first sight of it in 1921 was America:

> *I like America,*
> *I have played around*
> *Every slappy-happy hunting ground*
> *But I find America — okay*
> *And come what may*
> *Give me a holiday*
> *In the good old U. S. A.*
> *I like America,*
> *Every scrap of it,*
> *All the sentimental crap of it.*
> *I've been about a bit*
> *But I must admit*
> *That I didn't know the half of it*
> *Till I hit the U. S. A.*

'I Like America' from *Ace of Clubs* (1949)

:::   :::   :::

'Krispy-Kuts' will make his every meal a passionate experience, while 'Maltofoam' will ensure an ecstatic old age for his mother because it is 'The Beer with a Kick to it'.

Australia Visited (1940)

But while he might like *America* most of the time, he never ceased to be amazed at the more bizarre aspects of Americans and Americana in general.

I love the weight of American Sunday newspapers. Pulling them up off the floor is good for the figure.

Dick Richards, *The Wit of Noël Coward* (1968)

⁘   ⁘   ⁘

Without America we should have no Coca-Cola, no
Marilyn Monroe and hardly any really good
literature about sex.

⁘   ⁘   ⁘

Verbal diarrhoea is a major defect in many American
writers. They have learnt assiduously *too many words*
and they wish you to know that they know *far more
words* than other people and, what is more, long and
complicated words. This adolescent crowing becomes
quite deafening sometimes and gets between them
and what they are trying to say . . .

Diaries (1955)

⁘   ⁘   ⁘

'It's strange to find an American who really loves
Jane Austen, isn't it?'
   'I don't know,' replied Lola dryly. 'She has
acquired quite an international reputation lately,
having got into the paperbacks.'

'Bon Voyage'

⁘   ⁘   ⁘

American women mostly have their clothes arranged
for them. And their faces, too, I think.

Dick Richards, *The Wit of Noël Coward* (1968)

⁘   ⁘   ⁘

Americans love ice and hate cold water and so the
swimming pools are as hot as *bouillabaisse*.

Dick Richards, *The Wit of Noël Coward* (1968)

⁝　⁝　⁝

It is really surprising how many American adults . . .
have plunged into psychiatry so that their egos have
grown inwards, like toenails.

Diaries (1962)

⁝　⁝　⁝

I hate the United States' behaviour to English, with
such words as 'hospitalized' and 'togetherness'. And
how about 'trained nurse'? Absurd. What in heaven's
name is the use of an *un*trained nurse?

To an American reporter

⁝　⁝　⁝

NORMA: After all, we all love our country and are
proud of it – it is the last refuge of peace and
freedom in the world today – but you must admit
that, once you've exhausted Palm Beach and
California, there aren't many places to go.

Time Remembered (1941) – unproduced play

⁝　⁝　⁝

MELODY: Americans have a passion for speed . . .
and yet no idea of time whatsoever – it's most
extraordinary.

Time Remembered (1941) – unproduced play

⸬   ⸬   ⸬

MAXIE: Buffet lunches . . . are always a drain on
one's vitality. They call them fork luncheons over
here, you know. I always think it sounds vaguely
pornographic.

Time Remembered (1941) – unproduced play

⁘　⁘　⁘

In America they have to be told what to enjoy and what to avoid, not only in the theatre but in every phase of life. They are told by television what to eat, drink, or smoke, what cars to buy and what laxatives and sanitary towels to use. They are allowed to choose, admittedly from not too glamorous a selection, what gods to worship. The power of individual thought has been atrophied in them by the incessant onslaughts of commercialism.

Diaries (1957)

But even so, when all was said and done . . .

> *I like America*
> *Its Society*
> *Offers infinite variety*
> *And come what may*
> *I shall return some day*
> *To the good old U. S. A.*

And he frequently did.

Travel was Coward's safety valve. When his pressured professional life caught up with him – which it frequently did – his recourse was to embark on a long trip to recharge his batteries.

I have never liked living anywhere all the year round.

⁘　⁘　⁘

When the storm clouds are riding through a winter sky
Sail away – sail away.
When the love-light is fading in your sweetheart's eye
Sail away – sail away.
When you feel your song is orchestrated wrong
Why should you prolong
Your stay?
When the wind and the weather blow your dreams sky
      high
Sail away – sail away!

       'Sail Away' from *Ace of Clubs* (1950)

⠿   ⠿   ⠿

When I'm feeling dreary and blue,
I'm only too
Glad to be left alone.
Dreaming of a place in the sun.
When day is done,
Far from a telephone . . .

I'm world weary, world weary,
Living in a great big town,
I find it so dreary, so dreary,
Everything looks grey or brown . . .

I can hardly wait
'Til I see the great
Open spaces,
My loving friends will not be there,
I'm so sick of their
God-damned faces.

      'World Weary' from *This Year of Grace!* (1928)

⠿   ⠿   ⠿

I have always believed in putting geographical
distance between myself and a flop.

Diaries (1948)

Much of his best work was done on the road to Samarkand (or somewhere similar).

> *I travel alone*
> *Sometimes I'm East,*
> *Sometimes I'm West,*
> *No chains can ever bind me;*
> *No remembered love can ever find me;*
> *I travel alone.*

'I Travel Alone' (1930)

The romantic in him liked to depict himself as the lone wanderer, the Flying (or Sailing) Englishman. The more mundane truth is that he rarely travelled alone but generally with one or more members of his loyal 'family'.

I love to go and I love to have been, but best of all I
love the intervals between arrivals and departures.

Present Indicative (1937)

⁖　⁖　⁖

I love travelling, but I'm always too late or too early.
I arrive in Japan when the cherry blossoms have
fallen. I get to China too early for the next
revolution. I reach Canada when the maple leaves
have gone. People are always telling me about
something I haven't seen. I find it very pleasant.

Diaries (1965)

⁝　⁝　⁝

Travel they say improves the mind,
An irritating platitude
Which frankly, entre nous,
Is very far from true . . .
There isn't a rock
Between Bangkok
And the beaches of Hispaniola,
That does not recoil
From suntan oil
And the gurgle of Coca-Cola

'Why do the Wrong People Travel?' from *Sail Away* (1961)

⁝　⁝　⁝

SEBASTIEN: And if you want a clear and concise
answer . . . about Americans being unpopular
abroad, I can give it to you now, firmly and
unequivocally. They take too many photographs
and ask too many questions.

Nude With Violin (1956)

⁝　⁝　⁝

In the course of my extensive wandering across the
world I have formed a strong aversion to tourists *en
masse* . . . I know that, ideally speaking, it is a 'good'
thing that people who have never set foot outside
their own back yards should be able to enjoy the
wonders of the world and I chide myself with fanciful
visions of sad little old ladies receiving unexpected
legacies and gallantly spending them on adventurous
travel. Unfortunately, however, very few of the old

ladies I have encountered on cruise ships have been either sad or little. On the contrary, most of them have been aggressive, full-bosomed, strident and altogether intolerable.

Past Conditional (1965)

⁑   ⁑   ⁑

There's nothing funnier than an Englishman travelling abroad.

Interview with Edgar Lustgarten (1972)

⁑   ⁑   ⁑

AMANDA: And India, the burning Ghars, or Ghats, or whatever they are, and the Taj Mahal. How *was* the Taj Mahal? . . . And it didn't look like a biscuit box, did it? I've always felt that it might.

Private Lives (1930)

⁑   ⁑   ⁑

I have not, as yet, seen the Taj Mahal at all, but I feel that when I do it will probably lie down in a consciously alluring attitude and pretend to be asleep.

Present Indicative (1937)

⁂ ⁂ ⁂

I don't care for China,
Japan's far too small,
I've rumbled the Rio Grande,
I hate Asia Minor,
I can't bear Bengal
And I shudder to think
Of the awful stink
On the road to Samarkand.

'I Like America' from *Ace of Clubs* (1949)

Travelling certainly had its downside. Having slept uncomfortably in a hotel bed in the tropics, he was asked by the manager if the hotel could put up a sign to say 'Noël Coward Slept Here'. He replied:

If you'll add one word – 'Fitfully'.

⁂ ⁂ ⁂

I wonder who thought of introducing leatherette into the tropics? Whoever did should have his balls snipped off and fastened to his nose with a safety pin. This should also happen to whoever thought of leatherette in the first place.

Diaries (1968)

⁂ ⁂ ⁂

Sunburn is very becoming – but only when it is even. One must be careful not to look like a mixed grill.

'The Lido Beach' from *This Year of Grace!* (1928)

Reflecting on a 1944 African trip:

> The Dinkas' claim to fame is that they are very tall,
> have the longest penises in the world and dye their
> hair with urine; doubtless cause and effect.

Future Indefinite (1954)

⁜   ⁜   ⁜

BRIGHTEYES: No hard liquor before sundown. It's a
   rule I learned from the tropics.
IRENE: Which tropics?
BRIGHTEYES: Palm Beach.

Long Island Sound (1947)

⁜   ⁜   ⁜

As I mentioned this morning to Charlie,
There is far too much music in Bali,
And altho' as a place it's entrancing,
There is also a thought too much dancing . . .

And altho' all the 'lovelies' and 'Pretties'
Unblushingly brandish their titties,
The whole thing's a little too clever
And there's too much artistic endeavour!

Forgive the aforementioned Charlie,
I had to rhyme something *with Bali.*

'Bali', *Collected Verse* (1984)

Once again, the telegram provided a concise form of communication with his nearest and dearest:

HAVE MOVED HOTEL EXCELSIOR STOP COUGHING MYSELF INTO A FIRENZE

Telegram from Florence to Cole Lesley,
Remembered Laughter (1976)

On another occasion he wired:

AM BACK FROM ISTANBUL WHERE I WAS KNOWN AS ENGLISH DELIGHT.

Kenneth Tynan in *The New Yorker* (1977)

An ardent visitor, Coward was a less enthusiastic host. If a guest was welcome for a return engagement, he or she would be played out of the house with a recording of 'I'll See You Again'.

The most beautiful thing about having people to stay is when they leave.

Volcano (1957)

Exposure to a lifetime of travelling finally caused him to ask:

Why do the wrong people travel, travel, travel,
When the right people stay back home?
What explains this mass mania
To leave Pennsylvania
And clack around like flocks of geese,
Demanding dry martinis on the Isles of Greece?

'Why do the Wrong People Travel?' from *Sail Away* (1961)

On his travels Coward was increasingly appalled by the mind and manners of his fellow travellers. In *Suite in Three Keys* (1965), an American lady tourist is complaining to another about her husband's lack of enthusiasm for seeing the sights:

> I managed to drag him into Saint Peter's in Rome and all he did was stomp around humming 'I Like New York in June' under his breath. I was mortified.

And the final verdict on the world according to Coward?

> My body has certainly wandered a good deal, but I have an uneasy suspicion that my mind has not wandered nearly enough.

Present Indicative (1937)

:::   :::   :::

> *Free from love's illusion, my heart is my own –*
> *I travel alone.*

'I Travel Alone' (1930)

PART FIVE

⋮⋮⋮ ⋮⋮⋮ ⋮⋮⋮

'If Love Were All . . .'

Coward's image seemed to suggest that the brittle should predominate over the more sensitive emotions, yet, when asked for the one word which encapsulated his life, he was in no doubt. Nor did he seek to wrap it in an aphorism: 'LOVE'. Throughout his life he was alternately love's willing and unwilling victim, and he found that fame was no defence against its slings and arrows. He summed it up most personally, perhaps, through Manon, the cabaret singer:

> *I believe in doing what I can,*
> *In crying when I must,*
> *In laughing when I choose.*
> *Heigh-ho, if love were all*
> *I should be lonely . . .*
>
> *But I believe that since my life began*
> *The most I've had is just*
> *A talent to amuse*
> *Heigh-ho, if love were all!*

'If Love Were All' from *Bitter Sweet* (1929)

⁑   ⁑   ⁑

To love and be loved is the most important thing in the world but it is often painful.

(1950)

⁑   ⁑   ⁑

How idiotic people are when they're in love. What an age-old devastating disease.

Cole Lesley, *Remembered Laughter* (1976)

⁜   ⁜   ⁜

Cruelty, possessiveness and petty jealousy are traits you develop when in love.

⁜   ⁜   ⁜

To hell with God damned 'L'Amour'! It always causes far more trouble than it is worth. Don't run after it. Don't court it. Keep it waiting off stage until you're good and ready for it and even then treat it with the suspicious disdain that it deserves.

Letter to Marlene Dietrich (1956)

⠿   ⠿   ⠿

My private emotions are going through the usual
familiar hoops, hoops that I fondly imagined I had
discarded years ago. I am sure it is good for the soul
and the spirit and the ultimate creative processes to
fall down into the dust again, but it is now and always
has been painful for me. My extraordinary gift of
concentration, which stands me in such good stead in
all other phases of my life, turns on these occasions
into a double-edged sword. My imagination works
overtime and frequently inaccurately. I scale heights
and tumble down lachrymose ravines. My humour
retires baffled (but not for long, thank God), and I lie
awake arguing with myself, jeering at myself and,
worst of all, pitying myself. All the gallant lyrics of all
the songs I have ever written rise up and mock me
while I lie in the dark and listen. It all has little to do
with the person, little to do with anyone but myself.
To me, passionate love has been like a tight shoe
rubbing blisters on my Achilles heel. That's of that. I
resent it and love it and wallow and recover and it's all
part of 'life's rich pattern' and I wish to God I could
handle it, but I never have and now I never will.

(Oi, Oi, that's enough of that.)

Diaries (1957)

But Noel could be positive about the amorous emotion . . .

ELYOT: Love is no use unless it's wise, and kind, and
   undramatic. Something steady and sweet, to
   smooth out your nerves when you're tired.
   Something tremendously cosy; and unflurried by

scenes and jealousies. That's what I want, what
I've always wanted, really.

Private Lives (1930)

⁘   ⁘   ⁘

Love is a true understanding of just a few people for
each other. Passionate love we will leave on one side
for that rises, gets to its peak and dies away. True
love is something much more akin to friendship and
friendship, I suppose, is the greatest benison and
compensation that Man has.

(1970)

Coward on love – and loss – is perhaps best expressed in his lyrics and verse,
where the 'secret heart' can express itself without self-consciousness . . .

> *Tell me, what is love?*
> *Is it some consuming flame;*
> *Part of the moon, part of the sun,*
> *Part of a dream barely begun?*

'What Is Love?' from *Bitter Sweet* (1929)

⁘   ⁘   ⁘

> *Some day I'll find you,*
> *Moonlight behind you,*
> *True to the dream I am dreaming.*
> *As I draw near you*
> *You'll smile a little smile;*
> *For a little while*
> *We shall stand*
> *Hand in hand.*

'Some Day I'll Find You' from *Private Lives* (1930)

⁙　⁙　⁙

You were there
Your eyes looked into mine and faltered
Everywhere
The colour of the whole world altered
False became true,
My universe tumbled in two,
The earth became heaven, for you
Were there.

'You Were There' from 'Shadow Play'
from *Tonight At 8:30* (1936)

⁙　⁙　⁙

This is to let you know
That all that I feel for you
Can never wholly go.
I love you and miss you even two hours away,
With all my heart. This is to let you know.

'This is to Let You Know', *Collected Verse* (1984)

⁙　⁙　⁙

Let our affair be a gay thing
And when these hours have flown
Then, without forgetting
Happiness that has passed,
There'll be no regretting
Fun that didn't quite last . . .
Let's say, 'Goodbye' and leave it alone.

'Let's Say Goodbye' from *Words and Music* (1932)

⁙　⁙　⁙

Things can't last for ever,
Lover's hours are fleet,
Destiny may sever
Happiness complete,
Passion's so uncertain,
Some unfinished rhyme
May bring down the curtain
Long before it's time.

'The Dream Is Over' (1920s)

⁙   ⁙   ⁙

Do you remember those exquisite
Oysters we had in Peking?
And the stale caviar
That we ate in the bar
Of the Station Hotel in King's Lynn?
What a sophisticated pair
And what a dull love affair!

'The Parting of the Ways' from *Sigh No More* (1945)

⁙   ⁙   ⁙

Where are the songs we sung
When love in our hearts was young?
Where, in the limbo of the swiftly passing years,
Lie all our hopes and dreams and fears?
Where have they gone – words that rang so true
When Love in our hearts was new?

'Where are the Songs we Sung?'
from *Operette* (1938)

But then, there was love and there was marriage – an altogether more questionable enterprise. On that subject – never having tried it – Coward was (at least in print) of one mind:

> OLIVE: Marriage nowadays is nothing but a temporary refuge for those who are uncomfortable at home.
>
> *The Rat Trap* (1918)

⁚⁚⁚ ⁚⁚⁚ ⁚⁚⁚

> RUTH: We've both been married before – careless rapture at this stage would be incongruous and embarrassing
>
> *Blithe Spirit* (1941)

⁚⁚⁚ ⁚⁚⁚ ⁚⁚⁚

There are many reasons why you should marry – for love or for money – and many why you shouldn't.

⁚⁚⁚ ⁚⁚⁚ ⁚⁚⁚

Table d'hôte is marriage.
Free love is *à la carte*.

⁚⁚⁚ ⁚⁚⁚ ⁚⁚⁚

She married in haste and repented at Brixton.

Line of unused dialogue (c. 1918)

⁚⁚⁚ ⁚⁚⁚ ⁚⁚⁚

ZOE: I must say I consider marriage an over-rated amusement.

This was a Man (1926)

⁘　⁘　⁘

TOBY: Marriage is a sacrament, a mystic rite, and you persist in regarding it as a sort of plumber's estimate.

'Ways and Means' from *Tonight At 8.30* (1935)

⁘　⁘　⁘

I consider boredom the most legitimate of all reasons for a divorce.

World Telegram (1931)

The simple fact of life for Coward was that men and women were two entirely different species, fundamentally incompatible and not meant to live together:

ELYOT: It doesn't suit women to be promiscuous.

AMANDA: It doesn't suit men for women to be promiscuous.

Private Lives (1930)

⁂　⁂　⁂

CICELY: Are you trying to drive me to my lover's arms?

GEORGE: I fail to see the point of driving you, dear, when you trot there so nicely by yourself.

The Young Idea (1922)

⁂　⁂　⁂

Why are men permitted to sin and sin again,
Say they're sorry and then begin again?
Have they certain glands that automatically combust?
Why is it accepted that they just must lust? . . .

Why are men acquitted of social treachery
When we women, with one light lechery,
Set our world ablaze?
Why is it the woman who pays and pays
To the end of her days?

'Why is it the Woman who Pays?'
from *After the Ball* (1954)

⁂　⁂　⁂

IRIS: I like men who go about a bit and see life.
LADY CARRINGTON: I suppose that's why so many
women marry commercial travellers.

The Unattainable (1918) – unproduced play

⁞⁞⁞   ⁞⁞⁞   ⁞⁞⁞

– I don't think my husband's been entirely faithful
to me.
– Whatever makes you think that?
– My last child doesn't resemble him in the slightest.

This Year of Grace! (1928)

Although he was perceptive in writing about women in his plays some of
his private musings would hardly have appealed to the Feminist Movement:

I can't think of one beautiful historical lady in a
position of power who wasn't a dithering idiot. I
suppose it's the beauty that does it. Oh, for the
humour and horse-sense of Queen Elizabeth I. I
have a feeling that Boadicea might have been fairly
bright but they were neither of them Gladys
Coopers.

(1969)

⁞⁞⁞   ⁞⁞⁞   ⁞⁞⁞

Imagine the chaos that would ensue if our destinies
were ruled, even temporarily by Nancy Astor or
Clare Booth Luce! Beatrice Lillie would be
infinitely less perilous. Some day I must really
settle down to writing a biography of that arch-idiot
Joan of Arc.

Diaries (1967)

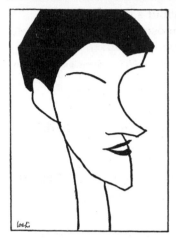 

Beatrice Lille and Noël Coward

In his personal life Coward adored women and wrote most of his greatest parts for them.

> RUTH: Your view of women is academic to say the least of it – just because you've always been dominated by them it doesn't necessarily follow that you know anything about them.
>
> *Blithe Spirit* (1941)

Nonetheless, throughout his career they were perpetual targets of his pen. Noël's descriptions of women were not always of the most charitable . . .

> ELYOT: Certain women should be struck regularly, like gongs.
>
> *Private Lives* (1930)

⁞   ⁞   ⁞

I have drunk from the Well of Truth and I feel it incumbent upon me to say that no man could possibly go on loving you after he had seen you in curlers.

Line of unused dialogue (c. 1919)

⁙   ⁙   ⁙

LUELLA: Is it true that Winnie Schaeffer is going to have another baby?

LESTER: She can't be!

IRENE: Judging by the look of it she didn't *quite* have the last one.

Long Island Sound (1947)

⁙   ⁙   ⁙

SHOLTO: I don't think one *could* go too far with Priscilla. She has no distance.

The Young Idea (1921)

⁙   ⁙   ⁙

SANDRA: Poor Cuckoo . . . She's not bad once you get below the surface.

BOFFIN: I'll wear an aqua-lung.

South Sea Bubble (1956)

⁙   ⁙   ⁙

JUDITH: I detest her. She's far too old for you, and she goes about using Sex as a sort of shrimping-net.

Hay Fever (1924)

⁙   ⁙   ⁙

ERIC: I don't think women ought to go on being
vulnerable after forty. It diminishes them.

Star Quality (1967)

:::   :::   :::

Her body had run to fat with such overdone
enthusiasm that she looked like an upholstered pear.

Beyond These Voices – unpublished novel

Not that male weakness fared any better:

> *Every peach out of reach is attractive*
> *'Cos it's just a little bit too high,*
> *And you'll find that every man*
> *Will try to pluck it if he can*
> *As he passes by.*
> *For the brute loves the fruit that's forbidden*
> *And I'll bet you half a crown*
> *He'll appreciate the flavour of it much, much more*
> *If he has to climb a bit to shake it down.*

'Forbidden Fruit' (1915)

True, the suggested wager of half a crown rather lets
down the tone. One cannot help feeling that a bet of
fifty pounds, or at least a fiver, would be more in
keeping with the general urbanity of the theme . . .
but this perhaps is hyper-criticism and it must also
be remembered that to the author half a crown in
1916 was the equivalent of five pounds in 1926. Also,
it rhymes with 'down'.

Present Indicative (1937)

Perhaps surprisingly, since he was homosexual, there are very few jokes at their expense – it was something he considered a personal matter. One of the few – probably because he found it impossible to pass up a good punch line – occurred when he visited Venice in 1936. Admiral of the Fleet, Sir Dudley Pound had arrived on his flagship. Pound and his wife decided to throw a party on board for the various celebrities who were in town and Noël and Lady Castlerosse were deputed to draw up the guest list. When they had done so, Lady Castlerosse looked at it dubiously and said to Noël:

> 'Noël, I have a dreadful feeling we've asked too many queer people.'

to which Noël replied:

> 'Don't worry. If we take care of the pansies, the Pounds will take care of themselves.'

⁙ ⁙ ⁙

Time and again
I'm tortured by contrition
And swear that I'm sorry I've sinned,
Then when I've lashed myself with whips and scourges
Sex emerges,
Out pop all the urges.

'Time and Again' (1955)

⁙ ⁙ ⁙

Sex and champagne as social institutions
Stampede me
And lead me astray

'Time and Again' (1966)

⁙ ⁙ ⁙

Freud could explain my curious condition
And Jung would have certainly grinned.
When I meet some sly dish
Who looks like my dish
I'm drunk – sunk – gone with the wind.

'Time and Again' (1955)

⁖　⁖　⁖

In cynical mood even sex was not all it was cracked up to be:

Sex and the weather have a good deal in common.

Observer (1969)

⁖　⁖　⁖

Travellers' cheques can
Do more than sex can . . .

'You're a Long, Long Way from America'
from *Sail Away* (1961)

Garry Essendine on sex:

To me the whole business is vastly over-rated. I
enjoy it for what it's worth and fully intend to go on
doing so for as long as anybody's interested and
when the time comes that they're not I shall be
perfectly content to settle down with an apple and a
good book!

Present Laughter (1939)

⁖　⁖　⁖

Pornography bores me, squalor disgusts me.

⁛　　⁛　　⁛

I think sex is over-rated practically everywhere – and sometimes under-rated. There is far too much nonsense talked about it.

(1969)

But sex could still be a source of amusement:

- A virgin bride shouldn't have the faintest idea what her husband looks like without his shirt.
- Bride I may be, but virgin comes under the heading of wishful thinking.
- I don't know what the younger generation is coming to.
- *I* do – and it's lovely.

'Bon Voyage'

⁛　　⁛　　⁛

SANDRA: Nothing has ever been able to convince the Samolans that sex is wrong. To them it's just as simple as eating mangoes.

BOFFIN: Only less stringy and indigestible.

South Sea Bubble (1956)

⁛　　⁛　　⁛

JUDY: You've no idea what you can have done to you nowadays, if you really put your mind to it. You can even have your sex changed at the drop of a hat.

NAOMI: King's Road, Chelsea must be knee deep in discarded bowlers.

Age Cannot Wither (1967) – unproduced play

Speaking more personally . . .

> I have enjoyed sex thoroughly, perhaps even
> excessively, all my life but it has never, except for
> brief wasteful moments, twisted my reason. I suspect
> that my sense of humour is as stubborn as my sanity,
> perhaps they're the same thing.

Letter to Edward Albee (1965)

:::   :::   :::

And yet in his more realistic moments he could admit that his emotional
judgements were often flawed . . .

> . . . something that I didn't myself realise at the time
> . . . was that apart from the swans which really were
> swans, I had a dangerous capacity for seeing nearly
> all geese as those beautiful birds: dangerous for me,
> that is – the geese naturally enjoyed it enormously . . .
> perhaps I have wasted too much time before realising
> that a number of them were not even geese but only
> lame ducks . . .
>
> There is a whole universe of difference between
> discovering and encouraging hidden capabilities in
> other people and over-estimating non-existent ones
> . . . Alas, it is a mistake we often make, especially
> when looking through eyes misting with love, that
> notorious impairer of hitherto perfect vision. Then,
> with our eyesight still off-true and rose-coloured, we
> heave the loved one on to a pedestal, an insecure
> lodging at best, and are unreasonably embittered and
> discouraged if the loved one should totter and fall.
> No, no – never demand from people more than they
> are capable of giving.

'The Best Advice I Ever Had' – Reader's Digest (1958)

As far as his own contribution to the Battle of the Sexes was concerned:

> I am the world's sexiest man . . . Indeed, if I put my mind to it, I am sure I could pass the supreme test and lure Miss Taylor away from Mr. Burton.
>
> Dick Richards, The Wit of Noël Coward (1968)

Noël was once being conducted around the red-light district of Honolulu:

> . . . when to my great surprise from an upstairs room in a down-at-the-heel bordello I heard the sound of my own voice singing – 'London Pride has been handed down to us . . .' I didn't think I'd be all that much of a come-on – but apparently I am!
>
> Television interview with David Frost (1969)

But – as was so often the case – the deeper feelings were left to the privacy of verse:

> *Time and tide can never sever*
> *Those whom love has bound forever.*
>
> 'Lover Of My Dreams' from Cavalcade (1931)

⁂ ⁂ ⁂

> *I am no good at love*
> *I betray it with little sins*
> *For I feel the misery of the end*
> *In the moment that it begins*
> *And the bitterness of the last good-bye*
> *Is the bitterness that wins.*
>
> 'I am No Good at Love' from Not Yet the Dodo (1967)

⁂ ⁂ ⁂

There's no more to say about love,
The poets have said it for ages,
They rhyme it with 'dove' and
    'above'
And praise it for pages and pages,
There isn't one passionate phrase
    that they miss,
Yet lovers find new ones each time
    that they kiss.
So what's a love poet to do
When lovers are all poets too?

'There's No More To Say About Love' (c.1937) –
unpublished song

PART SIX

⁞⁞⁞ ⁞⁞⁞ ⁞⁞⁞

'Sigh No More'

Oh, God!

That remark no longer has any dramatic significance. One uses it when one can't find a taxi!

⁙   ⁙   ⁙

My mind is . . . not really attuned to the Church of England or any other church for that matter. I loathe all that insistence on being a miserable sinner and asking for forgiveness. The traditional part of it is all right with the squeaky hymns and the choir (mixed) and the best bibs and tuckers and all the age-old carry-on, but the fundamental faith underlying it is missing in me. I never have felt and don't feel now the call of the Holy Spirit, and I suspect I never shall.

Diaries (1964)

Many people are surprised to find that religion – however disorganised – was a thread that ran through Coward's life. His attitude to it was at best ambivalent but, like a spiritual itch, he kept scratching it:

> *Do I believe in God?*
> *Well, yes, I suppose in a sort of way*
> *It's really terribly hard to say.*
>
> 'Do I Believe?' from *Collected Verse* (1984)

⁙   ⁙   ⁙

If I should ultimately meet my God,
He will not be the God of love or Battles,
He'll be some under God whose job it is
To organise sharp sounds and things that rattle.
He'll be the one who, all my life on earth,
Can, most sadistically, my spirit shatter
With little hammerings and sudden shouts
And hollow ricochets of empty mirth.

'Lines to God' – unpublished verse

His first exposure was early. As a nine-year-old child performer he was asked to sing anthems in churches:

But I hated doing this because the lack of applause depressed me. It irritated me when I had soared magnificently through 'God is a Spirit' or 'Oh, For the Wings of a Dove' to see the entire congregation scuffle on to their knees murmuring gloomy 'Amens' instead of clapping loudly and shouting 'Bravo'.

Present Indicative (1937)

⁛　⁛　⁛

I had a religious mania lasting exactly one day and based on an inexplicable fear of death which descended upon me abruptly in the middle of a matinée . . . There was thunder in the air as well, and during that night a terrific storm broke, convincing me that this was my destined finish. I wept thoroughly at the vivid picture of Mother's face when she heard how the sharp lightning had struck her darling through the window of the second floor back. I murmured incoherent prayers, vowed many vows and promised many promises, if only I might live a little longer. They were apparently granted, for I woke up the next morning as bright as a button and rapidly forgot the whole episode, promises and all.

(c. 1916)

At sixteen the contact with religion was rather more personal. In a 1969 television interview he told David Frost how at his Confirmation class the local vicar had touched his knee, causing Coward to remark:

Vicar, you are supposed to be preparing me for Confirmation. When I have received the gift of the Holy Spirit, if I'm in the mood, I'll telephone you.

Nor was this to be his only brush with the Church (so to speak). When the local vicar called at his Kent home early in 1946:

He talked a great deal of cock and never drew breath. Matelot (Coward's dog) complicated the interview by attempting to rape him. I removed him saying – 'Matelot, *not* the vicar!'

Diaries (1946)

Although he could reflect on God in the privacy of his *Diaries* or in verse, he became self-conscious when the subject cropped up in public. In the interview with Frost he was asked about his attitude to God:

We've never been intimate – but maybe we do have a few things in common.

. . . and when Frost pressed him on his personal visions of Hell:

They're all to do with over-acting!

(1969)

Nor was he averse to invoking the Deity on really important occasions. For instance, the afternoon nap was sacrosanct. He told Cole Lesley, his chief aide:

> If God rings, tell Him I'm not in.

Cole Lesley, *Remembered Laughter* (1976)

⁖   ⁖   ⁖

LEO: Doesn't the Eye of Heaven mean anything to you?
GILDA: Only when it winks!

Design For Living (1932)

⁖   ⁖   ⁖

LADY CARRINGTON: Prayer only becomes really
trying when one has linoleum in one's bedroom.

The Unattainable (1918) – unpublished play

⁙   ⁙   ⁙

She surveyed the house with a bright smile, the sort
of smile you receive from a Christian Scientist when
you announce that you have a toothache.

Beyond These Voices – unpublished novel

⁙   ⁙   ⁙

I don't know who it was who said, 'The only time I
believe in God is when I write', but whoever it was
said a mouthful.

Diaries (1955)

⁙   ⁙   ⁙

I have little reverence for the teachings of Christian
Science; as a religion it has always seemed to me to
induce a certain air of superiority in its devotees, as
well as encouraging them to swish their skirts aside
from many of life's unspiritual, but quite
unquestionable, realities.

Future Indefinite (1954)

⁙   ⁙   ⁙

Christianity has caused a great deal more suffering
both mentally and physically, than any other religion
in the history of mankind . . . the endless succession
of tortured, oppressed, Puritan-ridden generations

that have resulted from that unfortunately over-publicised episode at Jerusalem 1,995 years ago. I must say it is a little hard on Jesus Christ to be for ever associated with such a monumental balls-up

Diaries (1955)

⋮⋮ ⋮⋮ ⋮⋮

GRIZEL: God moves in mysterious ways.

LUCY: That sounds blasphemous.

GRIZEL: Nature, then. Almost every natural instinct we have leads us straight as a die to the most appalling indignities. I expect that's why all those dreary religious reformers carry on the way they do about sex being a sin and the life of the spirit being the thing to hang on to tooth and claw. They must be mortified every time they go to the loo.

Pomp and Circumstance (1960) – play version

⋮⋮ ⋮⋮ ⋮⋮

ELYOT: All the futile moralists who try to make life unbearable. Laugh at them. Be flippant. Laugh at everything, all their sacred shibboleths. Flippancy brings out the acid in their damned sweetness and light . . .

Let's be superficial and pity the poor Philosophers. Let's blow trumpets and squeakers, and enjoy the party as much as we can, like very small, quite idiotic school-children.

Private Lives (1930)

⋮⋮ ⋮⋮ ⋮⋮

You'll grow out of it, dear, it's only a passing phase like thrush or measles. Girls always begin with religious mania, then become atheists and after that agnostics. When these three milestones are past, one can comfortably expect to settle down.

Line of unused dialogue (c. 1918)

⋮   ⋮   ⋮

I happen to love life as it is and not as it should be and I can envisage no steady reforms of the human spirit and if, by some magic, everybody became spiritually impeccable, I am quite convinced that they would bore the b'Jesus out of me.

Letter to Esmé Wynne-Tyson (1952)

⋮   ⋮   ⋮

I knew, in my teens, that the world was full of hatred, envy, malice, cruelty, jealousy, unrequited love, murder, despair and destruction. I also knew, at the same time, that it was full of kindness, joy, pleasure, requited love, generosity, fun, excitement, laughter and friends. Nothing that has happened to me over the years has caused me to re-adjust in my mind the balance of those observed phenomena.

Diaries

In his writings – often through the mouths of his characters – he would speculate on the Great Mysteries of the Universe:

CHARLES: Life without faith is an arid business.

Blithe Spirit (1941)

⠿ ⠿ ⠿

LEO: Life is a pleasure trip
. . . a Cheap Excursion.

Design For Living (1932)

⠿ ⠿ ⠿

Life is nothing but a game
of make-believe –

'When My Ship Comes Home'
from *London Calling* (1923)

⠿ ⠿ ⠿

MADAME ARCATI: Time is
the reef upon which all our
frail mystic ships are
wrecked.

Blithe Spirit (1941)

⠿ ⠿ ⠿

'Morality' was not the word that leapt immediately to mind in conversations about Coward and yet he wrote *The Vortex*, he said, out of a 'moral impetus'. So what, asked David Frost, do you do with your moral impetus nowadays?

I give it a little groundsel and feed it gently – it does all right.

Television interview (1970)

⠿ ⠿ ⠿

Astrology. I wasn't passionately interested in whether I was a Sagittarius or Taurus. I thought I was just *me*. Which is a very Sagittarian thing to say.

⁙   ⁙   ⁙

LOUISE: Life is awfully funny, isn't it?
EVAN: Not monotonously so.

Long Island Sound (1947)

⁙   ⁙   ⁙

CLINTON: I believe that life is for living, don't you?
SEBASTIEN: It's difficult to know what else one could do with it.

Nude With Violin (1956)

⁙   ⁙   ⁙

Tout lasse, tout passe, tout casse. Life goes on and little bits of us get lost.

Diaries (1957)

Noël is here misquoting from Charles Cahier's *Quelque six mille proverbes* (1856) – No. 1718. It had long been a favourite of his but what he *should* have written was '*Tout passe, tout casse, tout lasse*' ('Everything passes, everything perishes, everything palls.')

⁙   ⁙   ⁙

The world to me will always be a gamble,
I don't care if I win or if I lose.

'Cosmopolitan Lady' from *On With the Dance* (1925)

⁞ ⁞ ⁞

Time, as I have so often wittily said, is a great healer.

Diaries (1963)

And as for humankind . . .

The human race is cruel, idiotic, sentimental, predatory, ungrateful, ugly, conceited and egocentric to the last ditch and the occasional discovery of an isolated exception is as deliciously surprising as finding a sudden Brazil nut in what you *know* to be five pounds of vanilla creams.

⁞ ⁞ ⁞

I care a very great deal about the human race; it is, when all is said and done, all we have got.

Dick Richards, *The Wit of Noël Coward* (1968)

⁞ ⁞ ⁞

I have no deep thoughts about the human race, nor am I particularly interested in reforming it; indeed, if I did, there would be nothing left for me to write about.

⁞ ⁞ ⁞

ISOBEL: Just fancy! One lives and learns, doesn't one?
SEBASTIEN: That's certainly one of the more prevalent human illusions, madame.

Nude With Violin (1956)

⁞ ⁞ ⁞

COLEY: Well, we live and learn, don't we?
NOËL: Yes, and we die and forget it all

Cole Lesley,
Remembered Laughter (1976)

⁙   ⁙   ⁙

Cole [Lesley] and I had a long and cosy talk
about death the other evening . . . we came to the
sensible conclusion that there was nothing to be
done. We should have to get on with life until our
time came. I said, 'After all, the day had to go on
and breakfast had to be eaten', and he replied that
if I died he might find it a little difficult to eat
breakfast but would probably be peckish by
lunch-time.

Diaries (1961)

⁙   ⁙   ⁙

ELYOT: Death's very laughable, such a cunning little
mystery. All done with mirrors.

Private Lives (1930)

⁙   ⁙   ⁙

The finality of death is bewildering on first
acquaintance and the words 'never again' too sad to
believe entirely.

Present Indicative (1937)

⁙   ⁙   ⁙

How little they had to fear, those Victorians,
compared with us . . . The idea of death had so much
more dignity and grace. Lovesick girls went into
'declines' and had a little calf's-foot jelly and expired;
poets coughed their lives away in sanatoriums and
died peacefully, murmuring lovely things to their
loved ones.

'This Time Tomorrow'

⁜   ⁜   ⁜

Death seems to me as natural a process as birth;
inevitable, absolute and final. If, when it happens to
me, I find myself in a sort of Odeon ante-room
queuing up for an interview with Our Lord, I shall
be very surprised indeed.

Diaries (1955)

At the end of the war the authorities came across the Nazi list of people to
be liquidated immediately Britain was occupied. Sharing top billing were
Noël and his friend, Rebecca West, who sent him a post-card . . .

MY DEAR, THE PEOPLE WE SHOULD HAVE
BEEN SEEN DEAD WITH.

The young Coward must have felt himself to be immortal but, as with
everyone, the passing years took their toll, and age became a recurrent
topic:

Time's wingèd chariot is beginning to goose me.

Diaries (1959)

⁜   ⁜   ⁜

How do you do, middle age?
Autumn winds begin to blow
And so
I'd better unbend my mind to you
Though you know
I'm not quite yet resigned to you,
More relaxation,
More ease,
More time for snoozing,
What consolation
Are these
For those amusing
Pleasures I'm losing?
Shall I survive this decade
Or shall I merely fade out,
Done for – played out?
What are your designs for the final page?

'Middle Age' from *The Girl Who Came To Supper* (1963)

It is said that old age has its compensations. I wonder what they are?

Diaries (1967)

⁖   ⁖   ⁖

MAUDIE: Who was it that said there was something beautiful about growing old?
BONITA: Whoever it was, I have news for him.

Waiting in the Wings (1960)

⁖   ⁖   ⁖

PAWNIE: I expect Florence will just go on and on, then suddenly become quite beautifully old and go on and on still more.
HELEN: It's too late for her to become beautifully old, I'm afraid. She'll have to be young indefinitely.

The Vortex (1924)

⁖   ⁖   ⁖

Advancing years may bring about
A rather sweet nostalgia
In spite of rheumatism and gout
And, certainly, neuralgia.

'Something on a Tray' from *After the Ball* (1954)

⁖   ⁖   ⁖

One of the pleasures of growing older is the realisation that to be alone does not necessarily imply loneliness. For many years it has been my habit wherever I may be, to take an evening off, to relax my nerves, to gaze objectively at the world about me and the world within me; to know, for a few brief hours, that no contribution is required of me, neither wit, wisdom, sparkling repartee nor sage advice. On these quiet occasions I am always stimulated by the feeling that adventure may be just around the corner; not adventure in the sexual or dramatic sense, but adventure of the mind; something to distract, an idea, a sudden flick of memory, an observed incident, trivial in itself perhaps, but sharp and clear enough to quicken my creative impulse and fire my imagination.

Beyond These Voices – unpublished novel

⁞⁞⁞   ⁞⁞⁞   ⁞⁞⁞

His advice to Edith Evans:

If a person over fifty tries too hard to be 'with it', they soon find they're without everything.

Attributed

⁞⁞⁞   ⁞⁞⁞   ⁞⁞⁞

I have never felt the necessity of being 'with it'. I'm all for staying in my place.

John Lahr, *Coward the Playwright* (1982)

⁞⁞⁞   ⁞⁞⁞   ⁞⁞⁞

Age is very curious. You must accept it yet ignore it at the same time. You should never try to be younger than you are.

Interview with Hunter Davies (1969)

⦂⦂⦂   ⦂⦂⦂   ⦂⦂⦂

HELEN: You're ten years older than I am, but when
   I'm your age I shall be twenty years older than you.
FLORENCE: *Darling,* how deliciously involved – what
   can you mean by that?

The Vortex (1924)

Trying to talk to Marlene Dietrich on the subject of old age:

I said to her, with an effort at grey comedy, 'All I
demand from my friends nowadays is that they live
through lunch', to which she replied, puzzled, 'Why
lunch, sweetheart?'

Diaries (1968)

Caricature by William Auerbach-Levy

· 136 ·

A few years earlier he had tried the line out on actress Benita Hume. At that point the meal of choice had been 'dinner'. Presumably, in refining it, he decided 'lunch' had a greater poignancy.

On his 69th birthday:

> I sat up in bed submerged in [gift] wrappings and looking like an ancient Buddhist priest with a minor attack of jaundice. One year off seventy now! Just fancy. The snows of yesteryear are a bloody long way off.

Diaries (1968)

:::   :::   :::

> Old age is cruel and death much kinder when it is gentle.

Diaries (1953)

:::   :::   :::

> Personally I wish only for ultimate oblivion, which is fortunate because I think it is all I shall get . . . Why not get on with the material and experience at hand and try to make the best of it? . . . I am neither impressed by, nor frightened of, death. I admit that I am scared about the manner of my dying.

Diaries (1955)

:::   :::   :::

Personally I would rather not wait until the faculties begin to go. However, that must be left in the hands of 'The One Above' and I hope he'll do something about it and not just sit there.

Diaries (1965)

⁘   ⁘   ⁘

I would prefer Fate to allow me to go to sleep when it's my proper bedtime. I never have been one for staying up too late.

Diaries (1967)

⁘   ⁘   ⁘

I'll settle without apprehension for oblivion. I cannot really feel that oblivion will be disappointing. Life and love and fame and fortune can all be disappointing, but not dear old oblivion. Hurray for eternity.

Diaries (1961)

Nonetheless, he did find compensations in the love of 'family' and friends:

> *When I have fears, as Keats had fears,*
> *Of the moment I'll cease to be*
> *I console myself with vanished years*
> *Remembered laughter, remembered tears,*
> *And the peace of the changing sea.*

Collected Verse (1984)

⁘   ⁘   ⁘

As one gets older people begin to die and when each one goes a little light goes out.

Diaries (1949)

⁛   ⁛   ⁛

The Grim Reaper has been at it again . . . One by one they go – a bit chipped off here, a bit chipped off there. It is an inevitability that one must prepare the heart and mind for . . . Those I have really loved are with me in moments of memory – whole and intact and unchanged. I cannot envisage them in another sphere. I do not even wish to.

Diaries (1961)

⁛   ⁛   ⁛

I can enjoy retrospective laughter again and again, but retrospective tears never. The eyes remain dry.

⁛   ⁛   ⁛

We shall still be together
When our life's journey ends,
For wherever we chance to go
We shall always be friends.
We may find while we're travelling through the years
Moments of joy and love and happiness.
Reason for grief, reason for tears.
Come the wild, wild weather,
If we've lost or we've won,
We'll remember these words we say
Till our story is done.

'Come the Wild, Wild Weather' (1960)

⌗   ⌗   ⌗

There is no sense in grief, it wastes emotional energy.

Diaries (1967)

⌗   ⌗   ⌗

I do not approve of mourning, I approve only of remembering!

But even so. . .

It is a natural enough malaise, this idealised remembering, but should not be encouraged too much. There is no future in the past.

Diaries

Noël died peacefully in Jamaica at the age of 73.

PART SEVEN

⁞⁞ ⁞⁞ ⁞⁞

Envoi:
'I'll See You Again'

Coward's best invention was himself. As the years went by he got into the habit of reviewing himself as though he were a character in one of his own plays – and, indeed, without too much of a stretch, he is to be found lurking inside certain of them. Garry Essendine in *Present Laughter* (1939) is perhaps the most obvious, and demonstrates the apparent paradox between the shy man and the show-off:

> GARRY: I don't give a hoot about posterity. Why should I worry about what people think of me when I'm dead as a doornail anyway? My worst defect is that I am apt to worry too much about what people think of me when I'm alive.

Present Laughter (1939)

Looking back on his life Coward could conclude:

First I was the *enfant terrible*. Then the Bright Young Thing. Now I'm a tradition.

Humble origins were most definitely de rigeur as the basis for a dramatic life:

I was truculent apparently about being born and made, with my usual theatrical acumen, a delayed entrance.

Diaries (1954)

⁛   ⁛   ⁛

Oh, how fortunate I was to be born poor. If mother had been able to afford to send me to private school, Eton and Oxford or Cambridge, it would probably have set me back years.

Diaries (1967)

⁛   ⁛   ⁛

My good fortune was to have a bright, acquisitive, but not, *not* an intellectual mind, and to have been impelled by circumstances to get out and earn my living and help with the instalments on the house.

Diaries (1969)

⁛   ⁛   ⁛

I have always distrusted too much education and intellectualism; it seems to me that they are always dead wrong about things that really matter.

Diaries (1967)

After a nervous breakdown in the early 1920s his doctor advised Noël to sit down and conduct an honest self-analysis of his strengths and weaknesses. He did so and called it a 'Mental Purge' . . .

DEFECTS

Over emotional and hysterical

Over anxiety to attain popularity

Jealousy fostered by over introspection

Intolerance

Lack of restraint – particularly emotionally

Self pitying

Predatory

Sentimental

Almost complete ignorance upon many subjects that I should know thoroughly, and a facility for faking knowledge

Physical cowardice

Histrionic in private life

Given to mental gymnastics at cost of other people's peace of mind

Domineering

Over emphatic in argument and practically everything

ASSETS

An excellent knowledge of psychology when
    unaffected by emotion

Strong sense of humour

Facility in conversation

Power of demanding and holding affection

Loyalty to friends and personal standards

Generosity and kindness of heart

Power of concentration

Several talents

Moral courage

Strength of will when unaffected by emotion

Common sense

Personality

⠿   ⠿   ⠿

If I'm in a group of people who are talking about
high policies, I have sense enough to keep quiet and
listen to them. And if they happen to be talking about
finance, I keep much quieter and possibly go to sleep.

Evening Standard (1966)

⠿   ⠿   ⠿

I was never, never in my life shy.

The Times (1969)

As it was he gave the journalists a helping hand in the shaping of the
appropriate persona, and charted not only where he intended to go but
also how to get there.

I am determined to travel through life first class.

Dick Richards, *The Wit of Noël Coward* (1968)

:::   :::   :::

I am related to no one except myself.

Press conference (1920)

:::   :::   :::

I've got an unworthy passion for popularity.

Easy Virtue (1923)

:::   :::   :::

I have always prided myself on my capacity for being just one jump ahead of what everybody expects of me.

. . . and if the jump didn't always succeed . . .

We must press on and rise above it.

He was also fond of quoting Milton's *Lycidas* . . .

> *At last he rose, and twitched his mantle blue;*
> *Tomorrow to fresh woods and pastures new.*

When his own career 'song' seemed to be 'orchestrated wrong' he confided to Cole Lesley:

I shall always pop out of another hole in the ground. I shall twitch my mantle blue, tomorrow to fresh woods and pastures new. Oh, I do wish people wouldn't always misquote that line [as 'fresh fields'].

⠿   ⠿   ⠿

If I don't care for things I simply don't look at them.

Dick Richards, *The Wit of Noël Coward* (1968)

And over the years there were a number of things he didn't much care for . . .

Most of my gift horses seem to have come with very bad teeth.

Present Indicative (1937)

⠿   ⠿   ⠿

I believe whole-heartedly in pleasure. As much pleasure as possible and as much work. I am very light-minded and very serious. I have no religion, but I believe in courage. I loathe fear and cruelty and hatred and destructiveness . . .

Daily Mail (1962)

Every now and again along the way the self-seeker stops to take stock:

SHE: I've over-educated myself in all the things I shouldn't have known at all.

Mild Oats (1922)

⠿   ⠿   ⠿

My sense of my importance to the world is relatively small. On the other hand, my sense of my own importance to myself is tremendous.

Present Indicative (1937)

Fame when it came was instant.

> Success took me to her bosom like a maternal boa
> constrictor.
>
> *A Talent to Amuse* (1969)

And since it came with *The Vortex* (1924), in which Coward played a young drug addict, the popular image was ready made and the 'effete young man' was happy to humour the Press:

> I really have a frightfully depraved mind. I am never
> out of opium dens, cocaine dens and other evil places.
> My mind is a mass of corruption.

Commenting (ironically!) to the *Evening Standard* on the press speculation caused by the opening of the play:

> No Press interviewer, photographer, or gossip-writer
> had to fight in order to see me, I was wide open to
> them all, smiling and burbling bright witticisms,
> giving my views on this and that, discussing such
> problems as whether or not the modern girl would
> make a good mother. I was photographed in every
> conceivable position . . . the legend of my modesty
> grew. I became extraordinarily unspoiled by my great
> success. As a matter of fact, I still am.
>
> *Present Indicative* (1937)

:::   :::   :::

> It's inevitable that the more successful I become, the
> more people will run after me. I don't believe in their
> friendship, and I don't take them seriously, but I
> enjoy them. Probably a damn sight more than they

enjoy me! I enjoy the whole damned thing. I've
worked hard for it all my life. They'll drop me, all
right, when they're tired of me.

> The prophetic words of Leo – the character Noël played
> in *Design For Living* (1932)

Whatever the subject, an interviewer could be sure of a quotable answer.
His idea of a perfect meal?

A little smoked salmon, a medium steak and perhaps
some onions and chocolate ice cream. I've always
been queer for chocolate!

His idea of comfort?

Good books, agreeable people and first-rate plumbing.

> Ed Murrow's *Small World* (1956)

The fact that he became a skilled subject for an interview never changed the
fact that he was deeply suspicious of the Press as an institution . . .

> *Let's fly away*
> *To where no threats of war obsess us*
> *And where the Press does not depress us*
> *Every single day . . .*
>
> *I frankly say*
> *I tear up each paper that publicises*
> *The rather uninspiring enterprises*
> *Of truck-drivers' wives who win competitions*
> *By photographing birds in odd positions,*
> *I don't care if a widow in Thames Ditton*
> *Plunged into a well to save her kitten.*

> 'Let's Fly Away' – adaptation of 1930 Cole Porter song

Was there anything he could *not* do?

> I could not dance in my own ballet.

On another occasion he would paraphrase . . .

> Well, I still can't saw ladies in half, or perform on the trapeze; but I'm working on it.
>
> Dick Richards, *The Wit of Noël Coward* (1968)

The unqualified success of the early 1920s was, in many ways, both the best and the worst thing that happened to him. The eventual dilution of it certainly brought perspective.

> GILDA: Success is far more perilous than failure, isn't it?
>
> *Design For Living* (1932)

Though the fame would continue unabated, the acclaim would never reach the same decibel level as before, and for much of the rest of his life Coward would gently mock his own image:

> In those days I was considered daring – now I'm practically Louisa M. Alcott.
>
> (1970)

There were occasional surrealistic moments when Fame seemed prepared to desert him entirely . . .

> The only bright moment in the hospital was when a perfectly strange lady with orange hair bounced into my room and said – 'Are you Miss Davis and would you like a shampoo?' I replied coldly in the negative to both questions.
>
> *Diaries* (1964)

Asked by luncheon guest, Beverley Baxter whether he had survived the war, he assured him that he most certainly had. On relating the conversation later, he told Cole Lesley:

Like Mother Goddam, I shall always survive.

(1946)

⁘   ⁘   ⁘

My face is not my fortune but it must be watched, if only for professional reasons. It is now all right and the correct shape, but it is no longer a young face and if it were it would be macabre. It is strange to examine it carefully and compare it with early photographs.

Diaries (1956)

He had very little patience with the would-be *enfants terribles* treading so rudely on his heels. In a 1932 song he could write that 'there's a younger Generation knock, knock, knocking at the door'. But now:

[I] cannot understand why the younger generation, instead of knocking at the door, should bash the fuck out of it.

Diaries (1957)

⁘   ⁘   ⁘

I like being chic. The young enchanters of today may have talent but why must they look so grubby? I think you should always look your best. I know it's not important but it's silly to be deliberately grubby. I've always had a feeling for being an attractive public figure. I would do nothing to spoil it.

Interview with Hunter Davies (1969)

During the late fifties and early sixties he was the target of much media browbeating – all of which he managed to rise above:

> It has been most gratifying . . . I now find myself as big a celebrity as Debbie Reynolds.
>
> Dick Richards, *The Wit of Noël Coward* (1968)

In this he was again recycling himself. In 1946 it had been 'Stalin and James Mason' – *Diaries* (1946).

> The only thing that intrigues me is that at the age of 56 I can still command such general abuse.
>
> Interview (1956)

⁂ ⁂ ⁂

> The battle, of course, will never end until the grave closes over me and then, oh dear, the balls that will be written about me.
>
> *Diaries* (1964)

⁂ ⁂ ⁂

> Whenever I reflect with what alarming rapidity I am trundling towards old age and the dusty grave, I find it comforting to count my blessings. And although the future, like the late Mrs. Fiske, is heavily veiled, my blessings, up to date, have certainly been considerable.
>
> *Past Conditional* (1965)

⁂ ⁂ ⁂

I'm not particularly interested in being remembered. It would be nice to have a little niche in posterity but it's not one of those dreadful things that haunts me.

⠿　　⠿　　⠿

I'm here for a short visit only
And I'd rather be loved than hated
Eternity may be lonely
When my body's disintegrated
And that which is loosely called my soul
Goes whizzing off through the infinite
By means of some vague, remote control
I'd like to think I was missed a bit.

'I'm Here for a Short Visit Only',
Collected Verse (1984)

Through it all he kept faith with himself:

The Almighty may write me out but I shall not write myself out.

Sunday Express (1963)

⠿　　⠿　　⠿

I'm an enormously talented man, and there's no use pretending I'm not.

Sunday Express (1965)

⠿　　⠿　　⠿

I think on the whole I am a better writer than I am given credit for being. It is fairly natural that my writing should be appreciated casually, because my personality, performances, music and legend get in the way. Someday I suspect, when Jesus has definitely got me for a sunbeam, my works may be adequately assessed.

Diaries (1956)

⁞   ⁞   ⁞

Really, my life has been one long extravaganza.

On re-reading his journals

Coward enjoyed the rewards success had brought him:

The world has treated me very well – but then I haven't treated it so badly either.

Ed Murrow's *Small World* (1959)

⁞   ⁞   ⁞

The public are very fond of me. I've done well by them, given them a lot. I'm proud that I'm popular and I've tried my best not to spoil it.

New York Times (1969)

⁞   ⁞   ⁞

I've had a wonderful life. I've still got rhythm, I've got music, who could ask for anything more?

Diaries (1961)

When his reputation was re-established in the mid-1960s, in what he gleefully dubbed 'Dad's Renaissance', he accepted victory with the same insouciance as he had embraced defeat. On the *Dick Cavett Show* (1970) the normally imperturbable Cavett was clearly tongue-tied in the presence of the abnormally imperturbable Noël:

> CAVETT: You're – you . . . what is the word when one has such terrific, prolific qualities?
> NOËL: Talent.

When the belated knighthood finally arrived, the investiture had an unintended touch of theatre that was not lost on the about-to-be Sir Noël.

> As I advanced the music changed from 'Hello, Dolly' to 'A Life On the Ocean Wave'.
>
> Letter to Nancy Mitford (1970)

⠿   ⠿   ⠿

My philosophy is as simple as ever – smoking, drinking, moderate sexual intercourse on a diminishing scale, reading and writing (not arithmetic). I have a selfish absorption in the well-being and achievement of Noël Coward.

Television interview (1970)

To what did he attribute his longevity?

To constant smoking and marrons glacés.

⠿   ⠿   ⠿

What – he was asked on his seventieth birthday – would he like as his epitaph?

He was much loved because he made people laugh and cry.

What were the two most beautiful things in the world?

Peace of mind and a sense of humour.

And how would he wish to be remembered?

By my charm.

His greatest single regret?

Not having taken more trouble with some of my work.

What was his idea of a perfect life?

Mine.

⁙   ⁙   ⁙

There will be lists of apocryphal jokes I never made
and gleeful misquotations of words I never said.
What a pity I shan't be here to enjoy them!

Diaries (1955)

⁙   ⁙   ⁙

With my usual watchful eye on posterity, I can only suggest to any wretched future biographer that he gets my daily engagement book and from that fills in anything he can find and good luck to him, poor bugger.

Diaries (1969)

⁙   ⁙   ⁙

My life has left me with no persistent regrets of any kind. I don't look back in anger, nor in anything approaching even mild rage; I rather look back in pleasure and amazement and amusement at the way my life has gone. It really has all been most enjoyable.

In a late TV interview he was asked to sum his life up in a single word. After an uncharacteristically long pause, he replied . . .

Well, now comes the terrible decision as to whether to be corny or not.

The answer *is* one word. Love.

To know that you are among people you love and who love you. That has made all the successes wonderful – much more wonderful than they'd have been anyway.

And that's it, really . . .